Anticipatory Grief

A Time to Grow Spiritually

By Virginia L. Campbell

Copyright © 2019 by Virginia L. Campbell
Contact: Virginia Campbell
Email: virginia@vlcampbell.com

All rights reserved. Printed in the Unites States of America. No part of this book may be used or reproduced without written permission of the author, except in the case of brief quotation embodied in critical articles and reviews.

Cover Photo by Ron Campbell

ISBN-13: 9781095389669

Table of Contents

Dedication	v
Prologue	vii

PART 1 Anticipatory Grief and Spirituality   1
    Introduction to PART 1   3
        Chapter 1 Anticipatory Grief   5
        Chapter 2 Decide to grow Spiritually   31

PART 2 Elements of Spirituality   47
    Introduction to PART 2   49
        Chapter 3 Spiritual Self Responsibility   51
        Chapter 4 Ego   59
        Chapter 5 Time   67
        Chapter 6 When to Die   73
        Chapter 7 Fear   85
        Chapter 8 Relationships   91
        Chapter 9 Love   99

PART 3 Elements of Love   107
    Introduction to PART 3   109
        Chapter 10 Grace   111
        Chapter 11 Compassion   115
        Chapter 12 Harmony   119
        Chapter 13 Wisdom   125
        Chapter 14 Forgiveness   129
        Chapter 15 Patience   135
        Chapter 16 Spiritual Courage   139
        Chapter 17 Gratitude   143
        Chapter 18 Unconditional Love   149
        Chapter 19 Service to Others   157

PART 4 Elements of Successful Spiritual Growth 165
   Introduction to PART 4   167
      Chapter 20 Successful Spiritual Growth 169

PART 5 My Stories   181
   Introduction to PART 5   183
      Chapter 21 Deacon   185
      Chapter 22 My Experience   193

PART 6 Deacon's Story by Deacon   199
   Introduction to PART 6   201
      Chapter 23 In the Beginning   203
      Chapter 24 French Fries   209
      Chapter 25 Snowbirds   214
      Chapter 26 Life in Idaho   221
      Chapter 27 My Last Days   229

Acknowledgements   235
Bibliography   237

I lovingly dedicate this book to my husband, Norm.

He has been my husband, protector, and
best friend for over 60 years

Prologue

Anticipatory Grief is different from the grief that is felt when a loved one passes quickly and unexpectedly. Sometimes this impending loss takes a long time. This period is often an excellent time to grow more spiritual. In addition to growing more spiritual yourself, you also become an example for others, even without meaning to. One might think that during this time of sorrow, grief, and frustration, it is not a time to grow spiritually, however often when times are the hardest, we are better able to learn the lessons that God wants us to learn. When everything is going our way, we get lazy and do not put out any effort to learn.

Think about a time that life felt like it was handing you challenge after challenge. Through these challenges you struggled, but you worked through them. Eventually you accepted them, even if for no other reason than to just get them to go away, and through the whole process, learned something valuable. Stepping out into the abyss of that challenge is when your growth started.

In this book we explore not only the meaning of anticipatory grief, but also what we can do for ourselves and others to turn this sorrowful time into a positive experience for all involved. As I was writing this book, God and His Universe sent me opportunities to experience firsthand each and every topic as it was being written. It was as if God was saying to me, "If you are going to ask others to do these things then you should also feel just how hard it is by experiencing it yourself."

The point is for you to see that each topic, although hard sometimes, can be accomplished through prayer, meditation, and above all, a desire to live a more spiritual and happier life.

Spirituality is broken down into easy to understand points with questions and exercises at the end of each chapter to help you integrate each one into your own life. You will see that as you practice, practice, practice, you grow more loving and kinder. As you grow more loving and kinder, you perhaps unintentionally grow more spiritual, and your soul grows more spiritual too.

God is always sending a stream of "well-being energy" to us, but if we are not in the right frame of mind to have our own spiritual energy at a high enough level, we will miss the message that God is sending. God loves us and never denies us his blessings. It is up to us to be in a position to accept and raise our energy up to receive these blessings. God has given us free will to decide for ourselves.

Practicing the Elements of Love during this period of anticipatory grieving will help you master each point discussed. This will often spill over to others in your life, and as they notice that you have changed, they may even mirror what you have learned. This may happen with or without them fully realizing that they want to be nicer, too. The atmosphere has changed and the desire for love of others takes over. As each person discards hate from their life and replaces it with love, the world becomes a better place for all.

The purpose of this book is found in the subtitle, *A Time to Grow Spiritually*. Although grieving through the anticipation of losing a dying loved one is the focus of growing spiritually in this book, it could be some other emotional situation that causes us to see our need to grow spiritually. Utilize this under lying purpose and the guidelines in each section to learn how to grow spiritually. You can substitute any other event in your life that takes a long time waiting for completion, such as a major, long-term medical condition, a series of multiple surgeries, cancer, slow healing, or complications from any other thing that constitutes a loss. Then apply the concept of growing more spiritual during this time of waiting.

    This information crosses all forms of religion or no religious beliefs at all. You can take what feels like truth to you and leave the rest. The Elements of Love which constitutes spiritually, are the simple things in life that make us happy whether we consider ourselves religious or not. I was raised traditional Christian and some of those are mentioned in the book. However, I have opened my heart and allowed more light from God to enter, and so have moved away from some of my early teachings. My own personal testimony is that I love God and His universe. I wanted, and have acquired, a personal relationship with God without the rules of established religion. You must decide for yourself what is right for you. When you look at the Elements of Love, which constitute spirituality, it is easy to see the connection with God.

    It is suggested that you purchase a three-ring binder to use while reading this book. There are exercises at the end of each chapter for you to explore your own life based on these topics. Taking the time to do the exercises is the most beneficial way to get a clear picture for yourself as to where you are in your life with each topic. Use this opportunity to put the information solidly into practice in your life.

This is not a book to just read from cover to cover and then put on a shelf. Take some time to read and contemplate how it applies to your life on a spiritual need level. Take this information and insert it into your life to bring more love and joy to yourself, your loved ones, and all of those around you.

How might you benefit by putting the suggestions from this book into practice? At the very least, it will make you a nicer person. At the very most, it will make you grow more spiritual. That is a win-win situation for you, your loved ones, and our planet. If all of humanity would find a way to become nicer it would raise the level of spiritual energy exponentially and the whole world would benefit. It starts with one person at a time... You. Believing and trying the information in this book is how it starts, and it grows through practice.

Try it... It is contagious, you will see.

PART 1

Anticipatory Grief
&
Spirituality

Part 1 Introduction
Anticipatory Grief and Spirituality

    Chapter 1 discusses differences between two very different types of grief over a loss: one that is sudden and maybe unexpected, and one that is prolonged. With a focus on anticipatory grief, this chapter suggests how to turn the period of grieving into a more positive time with a better outcome for yourself and your loved one. The things you learn and put into practice will enhance your happiness for the rest of your life.

    Chapter 2 explains that making the decision to grow more spiritual and focusing on it on a daily basis during this time, can also make the grieving process a more positive experience and helps you get through it gracefully. What is learned and practiced is something that can stay with you for the rest of your life and improves all your relationships here on earth as well as your relationship with God.

1
Anticipatory Grief

Life is pleasant,
Death is peaceful,
It's the transition that's troublesome.
Isaac Asimov

Losing a loved one is one of life's hardest parts of our life journey. When it happens suddenly, it takes away our breath and makes us question everything in our life. When it happens slowly, we have time to anticipate and assess what is happening and what is going to happen to us when they are gone. Which is better? Neither one! Both are hard to live through. Each one brings us to a different emotional place. Each one teaches us many of life's lessons; each also has the potential to teach spiritual lessons, as well.

In the pages of this book we will explore the time frame of grieving the loss of a loved one before they die. There are many good books written on grieving the death of a loved one. While I have read many such books, I see very little space devoted to the emotions that one experiences when the loved one takes a long time to die. It is usually only a paragraph or two in length. Most books are written about how to proceed with life after the sudden, unexpected death has occurred, which is important, however, this book will focus on how getting through the long-term loss is important to your well-being.

Grieving leads us down a path that can be considered one that makes us or breaks us. If we take the low road, we fall into blaming someone, something, anything to try to make us feel better. If we take the high road, we eventually can see the goodness in all that has happened. We can use this time to change our thoughts, which in turn, changes our lives. Both scenarios can be used by God to help us grow spiritually, if we let it.

Anticipatory Grief is a term assigned by society to identify the type of grief we have when we anticipate the loss of anything meaningful. It is the prolonged period before and while we are living through the agony as the loss happens. And yes, there will be a different grieving experience even after they are gone. We find ourselves feeling the impending doom and fearing the loss. It can be an object, job, pet, loved one, even waiting for healing (or not) of our own body or many other possibilities. There can be many reasons that cause us to experience loss. If we anticipate a loss, we may start experiencing or grieving it early on. We are anticipating the loss before it happens. Thus, you grieve for a very long time before the loss is completed and anticipatory grief is born into our lives.

As you read this book feel free to insert the loss that you are grieving, especially as you read the chapters explaining the Elements of Spirituality and love. Learning how to grow spiritually is not contained to only anticipatory grief over the loss of a loved one.

In this book, we are going to focus on the loss of life. Someone we love is going to die. We know that they will never get well again, and death is pending. But for some Divine reason, it doesn't happen right away. Some people move very slowly through the dying process, seeming to die by inches. Sometimes it goes on and on for what seems like endless tomorrows, turning into months, years, and even decades. We go through many emotions, anywhere from being happy that we still have them with us here on earth, to wishing the end would hurry up and come so this would all be over, and we could get on with life and perhaps someday be happy again. This wide swing of emotion causes an enormous amount of stress on us, from extreme happiness to extreme guilt.

At some point in our lives we will all experience grieving over the loss of a loved one. Not all will experience anticipatory grief, as it involves a long undetermined time frame before the death occurs. It may not be a spouse, but instead, any person that is very dear to us.

Grief mourning is an emotion that we feel when we experience loss like the death of a spouse, or another loved one. On the Holmes and Rahe Social Re-Adjustment Scale, the death of a spouse ranks at 100% as a stressor. In addition, on a continuum scale of negative to positive emotions, grief measures at the lowest point of negative emotions. At the top of the scale is most positive of emotions, love. We find that God's Love, in particular, is the highest, most rewarding, and most helpful aspect to lead us to have a happy life, even during the most stressful period of anticipatory grief.

The time spent waiting can be put to good use by focusing on growing spiritually. In fact, those of us that now find or have found ourselves in this situation can be sure that using this experience is what we, with God's help, planned for ourselves before we came into this lifetime, in order to advance our spiritual growth and hopefully the spiritual growth of our loved one as well.

Since grieving is the lowest feeling that we can have, it is seen as a negative on the surface but often it takes us deep within ourselves, which can become a positive. When we go deep within, we can find spiritual love, if we look for it. This spiritual love can uphold us during this stressful time of waiting for our loved one to die. Spiritual love can turn this time of stress into a positive.

In fact, although grieving the loss of a loved one does cause pain and suffering, we find that during the process the grieving can become very beneficial to us. David Hawkins (2002) explains his theory about pain in our lives. He says, *"Pain exists to promote evolution; its cumulative effect finally forces us in a new direction, although the mechanism may be very slow."* Viktor Frankl (1992) has this to say about suffering, which is what grieving the loss of a loved one causes, *"Man's main concern is not to gain pleasure or to avoid pain but rather to see a meaning in his life. Suffering is not necessary to find meaning, only that it is possible even in spite of suffering, providing the suffering is unavoidable. Suffering ceases to be suffering at the moment it finds a meaning, such as the meaning of a sacrifice."*

Is it not a sacrifice for one's self to give up a portion of their life while being there to support a loved one through a prolonged dying period? I believe it is, but it is a sacrifice that is given freely and therefore gives special meaning to the whole realm of anticipatory grieving.

How do we use this concept in our life when we are faced with such an awful situation of waiting? We can do this by focusing on spiritual concepts such as love, compassion, benevolence, forgiveness, harmony, etc. It doesn't matter what religious label or persuasion you have. It is not a matter of organized religion, but one of believing in a Higher Power, something bigger than ourselves. Trusting in what many call the God Power in Heaven which also resides within us.

All religions have a God, although different names or terms are used to identify this entity to those in their circle of friends, and acquaintances. Since I was raised in the Traditional Fundamental Christian Church with Christian concepts you will see some of that come through, along with expanded beliefs that are not part of the Christian traditional doctrines. But know that if you are already comfortable with a certain frame of reference for your relationship with God, then you have a pathway to greater spirituality in place for you already. This book will still be helpful to you to grow more spiritual during this hard time of waiting for your loved one to pass on.

If you do not know that you have a path to greater spirituality already carved out for yourself, then hopefully you can find your path through this book to learn how to become more spiritual. It will help you to have a better life, happier in all facets of your life, not only now, but in your future as well. Focus on love as the center of your being. Not only love of God, but love of everything surrounding you. You may find my first book helpful to better understand how God intervenes and helps us on our personal journeys. That book, titled *Spiritual Reflections...I Tried, God Helped,* can be purchased online at Amazon.com.

For me, these spiritual concepts have taken on a different look at times due to my migration or transition to more spirituality, which has allowed my Christian ideas to grow in new, exciting, and blessed ways. The boundaries are loosened, gates opened, and more spiritual light has come into my heart over the last fifteen years. Giving oneself permission to think outside the box of organized religion without fear, will allow more of God's love to enter your heart.

This book is not meant to try to convert you away from your current religious beliefs to be more like mine. I only mention the above so you can know from where I am coming. Wherever you are in your Godly beliefs, if it makes you happy and it feels like truth to you, then that is where you belong. You can still grow spiritually. We never really reach the highest level, while here on earth. We can always learn more.

Everyone needs to assess their level of spirituality, to assess for themselves, to ask themselves the question, "Just what is it that I do believe?" Traditional Christianity and related faiths look at God as our father (our spiritual parent). Followers of some religions have been taught to see themselves dependent on God for all that happens, good or bad. They try to obey and not anger God so he will give them goodness and reward their behavior. They worry about disappointing God. They are taught to be God fearing, when in reality there is no need to fear God. God doesn't want us to fear him. God is love. He does his work through love and only love. God loves us no matter what we do. God and his Universe are always working forces to achieve whatever our Soul planned to achieve before we came into this life.

Ron Campbell (2018) founder and Pastor of Small Group Disciples, has some thoughts on this subject and states that, *"This is the old testament way of thinking. For a Christian, it all changed with Jesus. His death and resurrection guarantee us a relationship with God, if they want it. And it also did away with all the old testament laws. In the Bible Jesus tells us to follow the 10 commandments, but there are two that if followed will encompass the other eight. They are, "Love the Lord your God with all your heart and with all your soul and with all your mind." This is the first and greatest commandment. And the second is like it, "Love your neighbor as yourself." All the Law and the Prophets hang on these two commandments." Matthew 22:37-40.*

For a Christian, God says in His Word (the Bible) that we are to be dependent on Him for everything. After all, everything belongs to God. He created it. However, He does not say that what happens to us good or bad is His fault.

The Catholic religion believes that we can anger God into making bad things happen and likewise if we are good… good things happen. The Mormon Religion believes in the same thing. Also, both Catholic and Mormon religions believe you can buy your way into Heaven by doing good works.

Christianity on the other hand believes that going to Heaven is a sure thing, if we believe in Jesus. This is His promise to all of us believers. The scripture of John 14:6 states, "I am the way and the truth and the life. No one comes to the Father except through me." Jesus talking to Nicodemus in John 3:16 states, "For God so loved the world that he gave his one and only Son, that whoever believes in him shall not perish but have eternal life."

Spirituality without organized religion believes that everyone came from a spiritual home and all will return to it. That spiritual home is Heaven. There are no rules to follow, just love God. In future chapters we will discuss this in more detail.

Pastor Campbell continues and gives us a different slant on the concept of fearing God in his online blog. He states, *"I often have people ask me to explain the fear of the Lord. My response is that fear in the Bible is an abounding respect or reverence and to obey Him. It means that you acknowledge Him to be your Creator and thus to have the right to be your Lord. It means that you act out of reverence for Him. It gives direction to your life. It leads to salvation."* He continues to list several scriptures that are full of examples of how fearing God is a positive rather than a negative thing. See Genesis 42:18, Exodus 9:29-31, Exodus 18:21, Matthew 10:28, 2 Corinthians 7:1, and Romans 3:18.

If this is a subject you are interested in, and decide to read these scriptures, try to replace the word "Fear" with "Respect" or "Have Reverence for." Pay attention to your feelings and see if it feels better to think of having reverence or respect for God instead of fearing Him. For example, Proverbs 9:10 (NKJV) would read like this: "The (fear) Respect of the Lord is the beginning of wisdom, and the knowledge of the Holy One is understanding."

Pastor Campbell goes on to say that, *"when one is replacing "Fear" with "Respect" we have to understand this is a respect that goes far beyond human understanding... the only way I can explain it is... It's a respect for God... So big, so enormous, so humbling that you would never, ever think of running away from Him. The only way to truly understand this kind of respect is through knowing God in an intimate personal relationship."*

Many people are moving to a more independent and self-responsible type of spirituality. It certainly doesn't leave God out, they just become more responsible for themselves as they honor God. They are building a closer, intimate relationship with God. They learn that they had a part in making the plan for their life and therefore are responsible for what is happening to them. They still honor God, perhaps more so than ever before in their life, as they really get to know God, not just the Bible. God allows us free choice but loves us no matter what choices are chosen. If we choose something that is not good for us, God leads us to try again, with no anger or disappointment on God's part. After a while, we learn what works for us and what doesn't. Never worry about the mistakes that you made in your choices, because mistakes make masters over time, if you use them to do differently next time you are confronted with making a choice on the same subject.

Grief is universal. Love is universal. Even Atheists experience these emotions and the stresses of anticipating the loss of a relationship through the death of a loved one. They too, look for ways to help themselves get through this anticipatory grieving in their life, although they may not think that spirituality is the way for them. Certain spiritual elements could still help them have a happier life. Just because they are Atheist doesn't mean they don't care, show compassion, and love those around them. They can still practice the Elements of Love and improve their lives. God loves them, even if they don't acknowledge and love God.

It is possible for everyone to turn a negative, like a loved one taking a long time to die, into a positive. Deciding to grow more spiritual is always a positive thing. This book focuses on spirituality as a means to turn this time into a positive. God and His Universe will help. Will it be easy? The answer is a resounding "NO." In fact, it may be the hardest thing you will ever experience. It takes strength and courage to pull yourself up from the depths that grief can take us. But it is always do-able and brings us so many rewards. You will see that it is well worth the effort.

Grief is an emotion that causes us to feel sad. Sadness can be detrimental to our well-being or it can help move us along on our journey. Society says we must grieve the loss of a loved one and we all most likely will. But underneath all the sadness when your loved one finally does die, we can also have joy because their struggle is over, and joy for ourselves when we realize how much we have grown spiritually through the process.

For the patient, the joy in living the active life they once had has been gone for a long time. Dying by inches is emotionally hard and sad in its own right. When they do pass on, we can be happy for them that they are no longer in pain or frustrated with their body and their lives. During this long period of time, they too grieve the loss of the life, the body, the roles they played in life, and they suffer sadness along with their loved one who is caring for them. We are giving up one person (them) but they are giving up everyone and everything they love. They see their family grieving and often try to become the strong one to make it easier for everyone. They accept their impending death and expand their capacity to love others and make the end of the journey easier for themselves and their loved ones.

They too chose this situation of taking a long time to die before they came into this life. This was something their soul wanted to experience to help their soul grow spiritually. They are not really victims; they are not being punished by God. It is happening due to a choice their soul made long ago in order to experience this scenario. Their soul is growing even if we can't see it on the surface while on our earthly plane. Sherrie Dillard (2017), explains that, *"Entering into the spiritual realm as unencumbered and free as possible from unfinished business allows the soul to ascend into higher vibrations of blissful cosmic love."* They are just taking a long time to finish their business of experiencing dying.

In 1969, Elizabeth Kubler-Ross gave us the steps to grieving based on her research on death and dying. These steps come from a reflection of grieving over patients who had been diagnosed with terminal illness. It appears that each of us go through these steps; however, the length of time and depth of emotion can vary from person to person. Each person mourns in their own way and length of time. The steps are:

1.	2.	3.	4.	5.
Shock	Denial	Anger	Depression	Integration, Adjustment, Transition

Shock is the first emotion we sense. This is often true even when death is prolonged. Many people who have gone through years and years of waiting, caring, and grieving are shocked when the time of death finally comes. They often voice how "fast" it happened, even if it took decades to happen. All five steps are in play whether the situation is sudden or prolonged, as in the case of anticipatory grieving.

Denial is also an emotion experienced when death finally comes, even throughout long-term anticipation of death. Often the survivor finds it hard to believe that the heart has finally stopped and their loved one, the person they have been caring for and grieving for so long, is now dead. They want the medical personnel to be sure the heart has stopped before they will let the paramedics or funeral home personnel take their loved one from the room. For some, it is very hard to give up the body.

Spending some time alone with the deceased loved one's body before it is taken away is usually very healing for many. If spending time with them is something that you desire, use this time to express your feelings to them. They can hear you from their new spiritual body. Do as you feel best for yourself and your loved one. Don't let anyone force you to do something you are not comfortable doing or not doing. Each loved one should be allowed to spend some time alone with the decedent if they desire to, before they take the body away. It is a reverent, peaceful, and loving time — one that will help each remaining person to move forward in their own grieving process.

Anger comes next. At some point those left behind will go through the emotional step of anger. They may be angry at the loved one that just died; angry for the long wait, for taking a big chunk of their own lives from them. Perhaps they are angry at being left alone to go on in life without their loved one at their side and they feel abandoned. Perhaps the anger is directed at medical personnel for not preventing this situation. Perhaps they are angry at themselves for not doing a better job at caring for their loved one or for wanting the situation to be over sooner. Then there are those that are angry at God for allowing all that has happened. These are all normal feelings. Do not be too hard on yourself or others. It is what it is! It will be best if you can accept that God had a hand in this and also the soul of the loved one that died was ready to go. They had done everything that the soul had wanted to accomplish in their lifetime.

The next step is depression, so be ready for it. You may feel like you have become "robotic" just going through the motions of living day after day for endless tomorrows. This is normal for grieving before or after the death occurs and especially during anticipatory grieving. Try to continue to go forward even during the anticipatory grieving time. Try to lessen the length of time you are depressed.

While we realize the reality of the situation and know we cannot turn the clock back, we also know we must pick up the pieces and move forward in life. Give yourself all the time needed, but also include times when you are trying to go forward. See friends, go to events, push yourself gently. This is normal for grieving.

It helps to have a plan of what life will be like after you are alone. Now is the time to look at that plan again, the one you set aside. Look at that plan often and work your way through it now that the plan can be put into play. This way you will advance on to step 5, Integration, Adjustment, and Transition.

Integration, Adjustment, and Transition is the goal to get your life going again. Now is the time to put your plan into action. Will it be easy? No, of course not. It is never easy to re-invent yourself. But, re-inventing yourself is what is necessary when they are gone. When you realize that you are a capable, intelligent person that can also function independently of your loved one, you will feel good about your successes in this endeavor. Your loved one is watching and trying to help you from their Heavenly home. They are sending you their love and protection. The more time you take to move through the grieving steps the longer they stay in close contact and they may not be "getting on" with all they have to do over there in Heaven. Release them to go and do the things they need to do in their new home as soon as you can. You can do this by saying (silently or out loud) what you want them to know. They are listening. They are watching you. Communication will be telepathic now.

Sameet M. Kumar, PH.D. (2005) uses an analogy of the experience of grief by thinking of it as a journey through a labyrinth. *"In Medieval Europe, many builders of churches and cathedrals created labyrinths on their grounds as places of pilgrimage. The labyrinth was intended to embody the pilgrimage to the Holy Land, which was too far for most Europeans to travel at that time. Labyrinths were also used by Native Americans to represent spiritual quests. A labyrinth is a complex winding path, often circular in shape, that you walk. The path usually leads you to a wider open area in the center that may contain a small garden or a bench for contemplation and rest. Reaching this area is the goal of your spiritual quest. As you walk the path of the labyrinth, you meditate on a problem or you repeat prayers."* Your quest too, can be to grow spiritually through the labyrinth of anticipatory grief.

The labyrinth is very complex so you can't see too far ahead. This is unlike a maze which typically contains dead ends. You cannot get lost in a labyrinth as long as you stay on the path. Just when you think you are lost or are never going to arrive you find yourself going straight to the center or heart of the labyrinth, a place of openness and calm.

The grieving process is much like the labyrinth. Anticipatory grieving is just starting the grieving process early on and the labyrinth is larger in that the path is longer. Your soul is growing in this process and bringing along the physical, emotional and spiritual aspects of your earthy body and mind. Be open to look for the good that is surely there. Ask God to help you find the good in this situation.

Grief is a state of distorted energy that can last for years, especially when the loved one doesn't die when it was expected they would. You know their death is coming, but it doesn't. The anticipation becomes an endless waiting game. This can, however, have a "good" side to it. The challenge during this time is to think of it as a blessing, even a multitude of blessings, because of the amount of time before death comes gives you time to focus on some special things to say to each other. Do this even if you are the only one able to say them.

Ira Byock, MD (1997) has shared extensively about the topics that need to be covered now to facilitate closure after your loved one has gone. The anticipatory grief timeframe allows us the time to do this. It is a true blessing to have this time. The following topics have been suggested:

1.	2.	3.	4.	5.
I'm Sorry	*I Forgive You*	*I Love You*	*Thank You*	*Good-bye*

Be thankful that you have this time. These things can be talked about over weeks or months as the occasion comes up naturally. They cover all the emotional areas of relationships. If we used the first one more often, all of our relationships would be better.

Should you not be able to cover these topics before death, know that both of you can still experience the healing effects through symbolically expressing them in a letter, art, poems or in meditation. Talk directly to your loved one even though they are gone. They can hear you. Some of you will hear them back.

Dr. Byock gives us some insight as to how these topics will help.

- *"I'm sorry" paves the way to forgiveness, for yourself and others."*
- *"I forgive you" doesn't mean that you will forget them, but forgive them. When you use compassion, this power helps you to release the hold that the issues had on your life."*
- *"I love you" is so essential because love is the greatest power of all. You cannot grieve without love first. Love is why you are grieving. Affirming this to someone opens your capacity to share yourself with another human being."*
- *"Thank you" is so necessary for what was special to you that you learned from the person."*
- *"Good-bye." When is the right time? You will know."*

The following poem crossed my path while researching this subject. Its author is unknown, but it expresses how grief can affect our emotions and how it is different for each person experiencing this difficult time in their life.

Grief

I had my own notion of grief.
I thought it was the sad time that
followed the death of someone you loved,
and you had to push through it to get to the other side.

But I'm learning there is no other side.
There is no pushing through.
But rather there is absorption,
Adjustment and acceptance.

Grief is not something you complete,
but rather, you endure It.

Grief is not a task to finish and move on,
but an element of yourself,
an alteration of your being.

A new way of seeing.
A new definition of self.

                                Author Unknown

However, when dealing with anticipatory grief, it does come to an end when the loved one dies. Then another type of grief takes over. One might think that since so much grieving had already taken place, so many tears shed, that there would not be any more grieving needing to take place. This is not the case in most situations. It has been said that grief never leaves you, it only changes as the unknown author above so eloquently told us.

Equally true is the fact that no one understands grieving until it is their own experience. There is no script to follow. There is no right or wrong. Only grieving can heal grief; the passage of time will lessen the acuteness, but time alone without the direct experience of grief, will not heal it.

There often is a path that anticipatory grief takes. It starts with a person deciding there is a problem with their health. They may deny that there is anything wrong for a while, but eventually they seek medical advice. Often, they deny the seriousness of the symptoms. Fear of facing death or long-term treatment is paramount, but usually denied. Anticipatory grief sets in when they and their loved ones realize the potential loss, including loss of health, mobility, and their future which cannot be denied any longer.

This first realization is a difficult time for both patient and their loved ones. Often family and close friends are brought into the issue and questions of whether to seek a cure and/or try to extend life as long as possible. When this goes on for a very long time, the ones that were so supportive eventually pull back and go on with their own lives. The patient and the care giver must cope with this issue but with less support. As the patient becomes more disabled, family and friends are called on to help more and more. This is hard on the supporters as their lives are disrupted too and their plans are contingent on the patient's illness.

A very slow decline may cause those closest to the patient to experience a sense of relief along with grief as death draws closer and closer and it appears that the ordeal is almost over. It is important to know that having these feelings of relief are normal, yet it may bring on significant guilt when the time of death finally comes.

Sometimes, to the surprise and delight of all, there may be a period when the illness has receded, and life can get back to normal again. Quite often this is short-lived or happens over and over again. With each symptom or pain that returns, it brings fear to all concerned. Each time it happens the whole process must be relived over and over again until the patient finally dies. This is quite prevalent in anticipatory grief and very hard on everyone it touches.

Eventually the terminal phase comes and most, if not all, accept it—including the patient. Comfort is the goal at this time. Tying up loose ends on personal desires and decisions should be completed and shared with all concerned. Does the patient want cremation or burial? Will there be an open or closed casket? The patient may want to say who gets their belongings. A to-do list should be made and then followed once the patient is gone. The location of the Will, if there is one, should also be disclosed. If there isn't a Will, then that process should be attended to immediately. Other important papers, such as life insurances, bills, bank deposit box keys, and money should all be located while the patient is able to participate. This should all happen long before the patient dies or becomes incapacitated, whenever possible.

Although these phases can be reassuring, they can also be a little misleading because grief, anticipatory grief and sudden death grief are never cut and dried. There is really no set structure to the process, yet it is still good to analyze. Grief is difficult for each person, often in different ways. The intensity can increase and decrease from one phase to another and even fluctuate within a phase. Additionally, after the death occurs a whole new path emerges. The transient nature of grief is part of what makes it so challenging. Kenneth Doka, Ph.D. and Joyce Davidson have dealt with this subject in more depth in their book, "Living with Grief." Some of their concepts are paraphrased above.

Anticipatory grief plays a central role in the grieving process. It helps us to accomplish two critical psychological tasks: 1) to understand that your loved one might not live, and 2) to prepare your mind for a future without your loved one in it.

It serves as a time to prepare yourself for your loved one's death on the mental, emotional, spiritual and physical levels. Anticipatory grief is as natural as grief in general. It is difficult to focus clearly on the here and now because you are always waiting for the future to happen. Even after the death, you will grieve, at least for a while. The hope is that it will be shorter since so much grieving has already been experienced before death.

However, this is not the case sometimes. Feelings of guilt sometimes must be dealt with over wanting it to be over quicker, as well as, feelings of being left out in the cold of what you wanted for your own future, especially if you are already a senior citizen. As this grief continues to be measured by years instead of weeks or months, you see yourself getting older too. You might feel that you physically can't do as much, for example, travelling, joining friends at evening gatherings in the neighborhood, or going to movies or eating out, etc. as this period of waiting drags on and on.

If you are young and have children in the home, you worry about how this long sad period is affecting the children and you worry about earning a living for your family and raising the kids by yourself. This is true for both men and women. It is so very hard for the physical ego to give up telling you that you deserve more for yourself. It can cause you to go to the negative side and resent your loved one for hanging on to life for so long. Growing spiritually will help you to stay positive. Talking with friends that understand and love you will help as well.

Taking each day one day at a time, and knowing that what you are experiencing is normal, you will eventually come to a better place emotionally. Divine timing (God's time) is in play here. We can either accept it or not, but if we turn to our spiritual soul and our God to help us through this painful time of loss, from beginning to end, we can grow in areas that one would think might not be possible. Turning to spirituality is like applying a soothing balm on our emotions. Yes, anticipatory grief can become a time to grow spiritually if we accept it as a blessing.

Anticipatory Grief is all about *waiting*. Those of us that have gone through watching a loved one die over a period of months, years, or even decades know what it feels like to have to wait. We ask God to hurry things up, then we feel guilty for doing so. We ask for patience; God offers it to us. We ask for understanding; God offers it to us. We ask for strength and love; God offers all of them to us through growing spiritually. We can accept these gifts from God, or not. If we do, we learn to know God in all His glory in a way that we would not have learned any other way. The following poem says it beautifully.

Wait

Desperately, helplessly, longingly, I cried.
Quietly, patiently, lovingly, He replied.
I pleaded, and I wept for a clue to my fate,
And the Master so gently said, "Child, you must wait."

"Wait? You say wait??" my indignant reply.
"Lord, I need answers, I need to know why.
Is your hand shortened? Or have you not heard?
By faith I have asked, and I'm claiming your Word.

My future, and all to which I can relate
Hangs in the balance, and you tell me "wait"?
I'm needing a "yes", a go-ahead sign,
Or even a "no", to which I can resign.

"And Lord, you have promised that if we believe,
We need but ask, and we shall receive.
And Lord I've been asking, and this is my cry:
"I'm weary of asking; I need a reply!"

Then quietly, softly, I learned of my fate
As my Master replied once again, "You must wait."
So I slumped in my chair; defeated and taut
And grumbled to God; "So I'm waiting, for what?"

He seemed then to kneel and His eyes met with mine
And He tenderly said, "I could give you a sign.
I could shake the heavens, darken the sun,
Raise the dead, cause the mountains to run".

All you see I could give, and pleased you would be.
You would have what you want, but you wouldn't know Me.
You'd not know the depth of My love for each Saint;
You'd not know the power that I give to the faint.

You'd not learn to see through clouds of despair;
You'd not learn to trust, just by knowing I'm there.
You'd not know the joy of resting in Me,
When darkness and silence was all you could see.

You would never experience that fullness of love
As the peace of My Spirit descends like a dove.
You would know that I give, and I save, for a start,
But you'd not know the depth of the beat of My heart.

The glow of My comfort late in the night;
The faith that I give when you walk without sight;
The depth that's beyond getting just what you ask
From an infinite God who makes what you have last.

And you never would know, should your pain quickly flee,
What it means that 'My grace is sufficient for thee.'
Yes, your dreams for that loved one o'ernight could come true,
But the loss! If you lost what I'm doing in you!

"So be silent, my child, and in time you will see
That the greatest of gifts is to get to know Me.
And though often My answers seem terribly late,
My most precious answer of all....is still... "Wait."

Russell Kelfer

At the end of each chapter there are some exercises for you to work on to help put this information into practice in your life. The hope is that you will find these exercises useful and that they help you evaluate your own situation and find your path to happiness, even during this stressful time in your life.

Keep a journal so that you can look back and think about your answers to see if they are still relevant after your loved one has died. You will be asked to plan for when this waiting period is over. Parts of the plan may change but, at the point that you can put it into action, at least you are not trying to start from scratch while you are moving through the grieving process after the death of a loved one.

It is also recommended that you create some affirmations. These are statements that can be used as a tool to help us change our core beliefs and live life differently. When they are repeated over and over, they become part of our subconscious and create new patterns. Say the affirmation on a daily basis or even several times a day. Tape them on your bathroom mirror, inside your kitchen cabinet door or wherever you will see them as a reminder. You could even make them into a screen saver on your computer. As we meditate on these affirmations, they become part of who we are.

Chapter 1 Exercises

1. This exercise is helpful to assess your own history on dealing with death of a loved one. Is this the first time or have you "been here before?" Doing this exercise will help you to understand where you are with this subject and why you feel as you do.

- Make a list, chronologically, of the times you have dealt with death of a loved one before. Take your journal for this book and write across the top of a page:

Identify Loved One	My Age	Sudden OR Prolonged	Reason for Loss (i.e., death, divorce, etc.)

   Doing this helps you to analyze your life and think about how you dealt with each sad and significant event. You may realize that you have done this before, sometimes many times before. It helps you plan how you will handle this loved one's death. It helps to see that grieving can help bring you closer to God and to become more spiritual. If you feel you did not handle your grief well in the past, list how you can do it differently this time?

2. Develop a plan for yourself for your future without your loved one.

- List where you will live, what will your finances look like and who will be in your support group?
- What is your greatest fear? Who will be your support system?
- Write positive affirmations to use to help you get through the first year. Read them daily or more often if they help you to stay focused.
- Often it is best if major moves and decisions can wait for a year. Wait until you have gotten your feet down and know that you can function independently. The time

warp that you have just gone through may continue for a little while as you go into a new way of grieving.
- Be gentle to yourself. Go at your own pace. Listen to others but go slow and wait until you are ready.
- Don't allow others to push you into something that you are not ready to do. List how you will deal with this, if and when it happens.

3. Ask yourself, "Are you afraid of God?"
   - Make a journal entry exploring your feelings about the "Fear of God."
   - Answer, "What does "God fearing" mean to you? Do you see it as respect or reverence instead of fear? How does it feel to change the verbiage?

Helpful Hints: List the ways that you are afraid of God. Analyze this list and determine if taking more responsibility for yourself spiritually and changing fear to respect can actually move you to a higher spiritual energy vibration and a closer walk with God. Can this also help you to understand that God always loves you? Remember, where there is Love there can be no hate.

2
Decide to Grow Spiritually

For the training of the body has limited benefit but Godliness is beneficial in every way, since it holds promise for the present life and also for the life to come.
1 Timothy 4:8

Many people, in fact most, eventually come to see grieving as a period when they experience intense personal and spiritual growth. This is especially true for anticipatory grief because of the extended amount of time involved. We can't change the time frame, but we do get to choose how we want to fill it. We can do it with love or hate. We can either utilize it for good for ourselves and our loved one, or we can cause ourselves, family members and our loved one more suffering.

You have the choice to "decide" to be spiritual when you find yourself in this space and time whereby you are waiting for a loved one to die. You know you should do something positive about this situation to help you get through it and at the same time, hopefully, assist your loved one to do the same. It is all a matter of first deciding and then activating that decision. It takes changing your own thinking and behavior to grow more spiritual.

Gloria Lintermans and Marilyn Stolzman (2006) explain that, *"Spirituality involves openness to something larger than oneself. This heightened state of consciousness may be achieved through meditation, nature, or prayer. While pondering the meaning of life, for instance, you may also become interested in understanding the nature of the universe. Spirituality is an indefinable experience and may occur when we see the ocean, view a sunset, or when we connect with another human being. It is a sense of renewal that comes from connecting ourselves to a higher power. There is a positive correlation between spirituality and recovery"* [from grief].

This extended period of grieving gives us an excellent opportunity to connect with God and the universe, or your own way of being spiritual. You don't have to have an attachment to a church doctrine. However, it is okay if you do. Everyone grieves. Even Pastors experience grief and struggle with how to move through it. Dr. Tony L. Nelson (2016), a Pastor of a large church for many years, writes of his experiences with grief when his brother died. He cites a verse from the Bible, 1 Thessalonians 4:13, *"Grieve with Hope."* Dr. Nelson shares his feelings when he says, *"I will always remember my loss, I have to let go of the whip handle of regret and now forgive myself and treat these memories with greater kindness. In the time since, I have stopped blaming God and let him off the hook, as well, learning a little more each day to take life on life's terms."*

Spirituality is a way to help you navigate through your suffering. It is not a cure. You still suffer loss. There is no cure for loss. You must go through it at your own pace and in your own way. Time alone will not heal it, but the passage of time will lessen the acuteness. Spirituality will help you feel better. It will keep you on your path to learn the lessons of grief and to become a better person during and even after your grieving is somewhat in the past. It will help you have greater compassion, forgiveness, benevolence, and mercy toward yourself, and your loved one that is dying. Compassion, forgiveness, benevolence and mercy may be the lessons that you are meant to experience and learn from during your lifetime.

Anticipatory grief allows us to do some of this healing before our loved one dies, often guiding them to grow spiritually as well, while learning the same lessons as they grieve their own death. Remember we are giving up one person and perhaps a way of life as we know it. They are giving up everything! Everything and everybody important in their life. They also may be experiencing fear of the unknown. They may have questions as to whether they will be going to Heaven or to Hell, if going to these places is possible in their belief system.

The following poem is written by my friend, Linda Erickson. She lost her little sister in 1986 due to cancer, the beast referred to in the poem. Linda very masterfully wrote about her grieving emotions, her pain, and her love in the poem. It took her seven years after her sister's death for her to be able to write this poem.

Thank you, Linda, for expressing your love, pain and grief over your sister's death and allowing me to share it in this book on grieving. Many will identify with it and gain strength from your words.

Sister

How could I know
    On that day
        When you were given to me
(Here's your new little sister.
    Don't hold her like that!
        Support her head, her neck, her back.
            Don't let her choke, smother,
                chill, sweat, cry.
                    Don't...)

How many times
    I would lead, dare, coax
        You into walking
            Strange paths
(How many times do I have to tell you to stay away from the
        Water, the woods, the fire, the roof,
            Insects, stray animals, machinery,
                Dirty old men, boys...
                      How many...?)
Into dangerous places
    Where you might have been
        Frightened, injured, killed,
            And, taking your life,
        Reshaping it before I gave it back to you,

That I would be so sure,
    So right, so strong, so infallible
        Until I engaged,
Armed with all of my knowledge

    And wisdom and will power and love,
        In hand-to-hand combat
With that beast who grazed so leisurely upon
    Your flesh and bones and hair and mind

(Take care of your sister,
        The tubes, the pads, the dressings, the mess
           You have made of everything)

Until there was so little left
    That I could easily hold you
        In one arm and support
The head and the back and

How many times could I have told you
    I loved you before
        You walked ahead on that path
           Without me.
                Linda Farrell Erickson, April 1993

All the different spiritual traditions have one thing in common, they all recognize the awareness of death. Death brings on grief, which can accelerate our spiritual development. When grief is analyzed from a spiritual point of view, it can be healthy. Healthy grief evolves when one is utilizing the pain that results from the loss, or potential loss, of a loved one, and trusts themselves to travel through the intense pain in order to re-emerge as a better person.

Approach your grief as an opportunity to grow spiritually by giving special meaning to your pain. During this prolonged time of anticipatory grief, see this opportunity as an extension of love, a time of opportunity to grow. See it as a time to highlight the depth of our capacity to love and be loved. Love depends on the courage to share yourself with another person. Grieving to grow spiritually depends on the courage to accept your own feelings. By focusing on growing spiritually you will find the natural place of grief in your life.

This book is suggesting that the perfect thing to do is to see this heart wrenching time as a blessing instead of a burden. Society tells us it is a time of suffering. This book is telling you that it is a time of blessings that could be used to grow spiritually. The Universe (God's Plan) is unfolding; it always will. It doesn't matter if you don't believe in God. The Divine Plan doesn't need you to unfold. If you turn away, it just won't unfold through you. You won't receive the blessings you could have and are yours to have. You will remain part of the problem of the world today. The choice is yours.

Deepak Chopra (2009) tells us, "*Do not seek out suffering in order to get through life's unforeseen and inevitable hurdles. Instead use spiritual growth to navigate* life's hurdles." He is telling us to decide to be more spiritual instead of suffering. Anticipatory grieving gives us this opportunity.

Linda Howe (2015) shares her thoughts when she says, "*Utilize your mind, heart, and will, which translates to idea, emotion, and action to make this decision, and carry it through to completion. It takes self-discipline to change something in your life. Decision making is an essential component of our spiritual evolution.*"

Ester and Jerry Hicks (2004) encourages us to, "*Practice the art of allowing. God sends out a stream of well-being, a stream of wellness, abundance, clarity and all good things that you desire flows. It is up to you to accept or resist. If you do not do something that causes a different energy vibration offering in yourself, then nothing in your experience can change.*"

Deciding to grow spiritually certainly changes your energy vibration to a higher level. One that makes you able to receive all of God's blessings. You may resist this stream of well-being from God; you have free choice from God to do so. Everything that happens to you is all your doing. That is because you are in control of your responses. God is sending blessings; you just have to prepare yourself to receive them. That is where your control comes in. You can resist or accept.

Perhaps you do not see yourself as particularly spiritual and yet this period of anticipatory grief is so very hard for you. You may feel anger often. You may feel like life is unfair to you and your loved one. You may be blaming God. The question, "Why me and my loved one?" comes up often in your mind. But as you analyze that very question, also analyze this one too, "Why *NOT* me and my loved one?"

If you look at what is happening to you and your loved one as though God is punishing you, then you need to forget the word punishment. God does not punish us he only loves us. In my opinion, that was the purpose of Jesus incarnating as a human on Earth. His sole purpose was to teach mankind that the God in the Old Testament no longer is and probably never was. God is a loving God. He has always been a loving God. Jesus taught us that, and also that the most important point is to love one another as we are all one.

We must focus more on love and not so much on how many souls will get into Heaven because they all will. Everyone came from Heaven and all will go back. That is what God's love represents. God is Love. Where there is love, there can be no hate.

Let's take a few moments to explore the spiritual spectrum. Included here is an abbreviated version. See Barbara Martin and Dimitri Moraitis (2006) writings to enjoy the complete explanation from the authors themselves. None the less, the following excerpt is taken from their book.

"The highest in the spiritual spectrum is God. God is the spiritual spectrum, and everything is part of God. Life begins with God. God is the author of existence and all that is life. God is the ever-expanding Eternal Creator of all that has been, is, and shall ever be. God is everywhere and in everything. God is Love, God is peace, God is joy. In terms of healing, God is health. This is why to connect with our source of health, we must connect with God. A step down in vibration from all-encompassing being of God is the intimate Spirit of God. Just as a drop of saltwater is part of the ocean, our spirits are precious drops from the ocean of Spirit. We are part of God's immortal Spirit. Our Divine Spirit is eternal and everlasting. Our physical form

will eventually go back to the earth from which it came, but our Spirit goes on eventually to the divine source from which it came."

"In addition to our Divine Spirit, we have a soul. Our soul is embryo of spirit. The soul has within it all of the God attributes of spirit, but these attributes are latent and need to be freely developed through the process of spiritual growth. It is soul that incarnates in flesh time and time again to learn the lessons of life. The spirit always remains in the spiritual realms to guide us, but it is our soul that embodies and interacts with the physical body and is susceptible to disease and illness. As we evolve, we raise our soul vibration and expand our spiritual power until spirit and soul became as one. This is the spiritual enlightenment that we seek."

Perhaps you have had a spiritual awakening already and just need to get closer to God to raise your spiritual vibration. Perhaps you have taken a pass on anything to do with spirituality. If that is the case, God still loves you.

Robert Schwartz (2012) explains what a spiritual awakening is: "[It] *is a deep, inner knowing that you are more than your body, more than your mind; that you are in truth an eternal being. Awakening experiences are planned in our lives* [before we come into this body] *and when we reach that point, we either accept or resist it* [the awakening experience]. *The repercussions of that decision, regardless of whether it was conscious or unconscious, will resound powerfully throughout the rest of our lives."*

Maureen Moss (2002) says: "*Courage is having the guts to go from hearing the message to doing something about it.*" She quotes author Henry Miller, in her book, *The Nature of Bliss,* when he wrote "*I believe it absolutely. I knew it from my own experience that all growth is a leap in the dark. A spontaneous, unpremeditated act without benefit of experience."*

While you are trying to grow spiritually, consider what Eckhart Tolle (2005) says as he shares his thoughts on his term of, "Awakened Doing". *"If you are not in the state of either acceptance, enjoyment, or enthusiasm, look closely and you will find that you are creating suffering for yourself and others. Acceptance means that you are at peace while doing it. Enjoyment replaces wanting as a motivating power behind your actions. Enthusiasm means there is deep enjoyment in what you do plus the added element of a goal or a vision that you work toward. When you add a goal to the enjoyment of what you do; the energy-field or vibrational frequency changes. A certain degree of what we might call structural tension is now added to enjoyment, and so it turns into enthusiasm."*

Traditional Western Christianity is full of wonderful examples of how we can live a happier life and be closer to God. But underlying all these wonderful ways is the idea that we as humans are not deserving of it if we don't "toe the line" in the Biblical way. Many spiritual authors call it the fear factor to get you to react the way your church wants you to react. Simple spirituality is free of those fears. It is just God and you. God does not use fear, only love and blessings.

Focusing on grace, gratitude and generosity will help you realize all the wonderful thoughts and blessings God is offering can be had easily. With each act of giving, you release one of the many sandbags that keep you from soaring spiritually. Actual giving (generosity) provides you with lift off. Those many sandbags are full of fear, guilt, shame and punishment. Let them go and get to know our real

God. It is easier to do this when we view our God as a loving God *ALWAYS* instead of our God being a punishing presence keeping us tied to a lower level of spirituality.

Staying at a lower level of spirituality is our choice, not God's. God wants us to be closer to him spiritually, not hold us back. He loves us no matter what we do, say or think. He is constantly trying to give us blessings but often we are not at the right vibration to receive these blessings. We have a loving God, not one that punishes us. He does not hold back blessings nor punish us in any other way. It is up to us to bring ourselves to a level of love of self, others, and love of God to receive his blessings; to allow them to come through our sorrow and despair. Striving to do this will bring us to that stream of well-being that God puts out now and for eternity.

Marianne Williamson (2004) explains that: *"The conversion to Christ need not entail a conversion to the Christian Religion. The word [Christ] is a symbol for the child of God within us, our true identity and a space of remembrance of all that is Devine. God's begotten Son is who we are. He is as clear in the Holy Instant [the second that you realize that you are in contact with God] as we allow him to be. Either he is metaphorically there or is literally there. Which it will be in your experience is completely up to you. In our one-ness with others lies our one-ness with God, and removing those walls is His work in us and in the world."*

We can start ourselves on this path or if already started, then move ourselves along faster if we start with our ego. That is because the ego gets in the way of spirituality. Without the ego all would be love. (More about the ego in a future chapter.)

Let me reiterate my point, you do not need to be associated with an established religion. You do not need to have rules to follow, church doctrines to worry about. Just love God. Read, listen and learn from books, classes, etc., but go your own way following God's love and have your own experiences. Some may see you as exceptional and/or eccentric. See yourself not necessarily following the ordinary religious behavior expected of those who follow the conventional religious observance of your country (whether it be Buddhist, Christian, Muslim or another organized religion) but rather, as a spiritual teacher to others of tolerance. You are giving them opportunities to have tolerance for some belief different than their own and opportunities to continue to love you as you love them back.

Please know that it is alright if you want to and feel most comfortable with one of the established religions as long as you focus on love and not on hate, guilt or fear. But know that those that do so are following a religion that has been made for them by others, communicated to them by tradition, determined to fixed forms by imitation and retained by habit. Established religion is helpful if a person is new to all kinds of religion or spirituality. But when a person already has a foundation, then now is the time to be like these pattern-setters were and find your own way instead of following a second-hand religion. William James (1902) goes into this in more detail in his book, "The Varieties of Religious Experience."

Speaking for myself, I prefer original experiences. I can only find these experiences when I quit following God or Jesus as a dull habit, but rather strike out and find my own way in the Spiritual World, one that is only between me and God. It is glorious! I would encourage everyone to at least explore and try to find their own way. God will lead you and protect you.

As you meditate, pray, and explore different religions or just follow your heart, you will grow more spiritual having your own Holy Instances, which is the moment that you realize and know you are in contact with God. Share your experiences as you want to or not. Make sure you are staying grounded and staying with love, coming from your heart. If and when you feel you are dipping into hate, guilt or fear, correct yourself and get back on the path to love and continue your journey. Make your own way with God. It is okay. It is good. Don't try to force it onto others as they have decided on their path and God loves them too. Their path is okay too as long as it is based on love of God. We are ALL ONE. It is not kind to push your religious beliefs on to others.

When you are living in a state of spirituality, it makes you more child-like in happiness and love. It could be described as a child-like innocence. Deepak Chopra (2009) reminds us that, *"In fact, only in innocence can you receive the gifts of the Soul."* Without the innocence of a child, we are more prone to worry and see the negative side of life.

While we are in the period of anticipatory grief we are vulnerable to have less innocence and to worry more. Deepak Chopra continues that, *"once you accept that you are supposed to struggle in order to survive, that becomes your reality. It gathers its own energy and momentum. Your brain quickly learns to conform. Once your brain is conditioned, the look, feel, and sound of the world have been fixed... until you escape that conditioning. By thinking that you must suffer for it, you are asking the Universe for it. You receive what you think about. What you think about creates your vibrations. Tune into your Soul and feel the innocence again."*

Anticipatory grief doesn't have to be all suffering. We can create, with God's help, a more loving time with our loved one. Yes, at times, it will be hard, but growing more in spirituality will make you and those around you suffer less.

Michael Singer (2007) tells us, *"When we analyze our position on spirituality it helps to first analyze the question, "Who am I?" When you contemplate the nature of self, you are meditating. That is why meditation is the highest state. It is the return to the root of your being, the simple awareness of being aware. Once you become conscious of the consciousness itself, you attain a totally different state. You are now aware of who you are. You have become an awakened being."* He continues to explain that when you can say, *"Here I am. Here I always was." You woke up... that is Spirituality. That is the nature of self. That is who you are."*

We realize as we meditate deeper and deeper the world is no longer a problem. Politics, money, weather, job, it all ceases to be of concern any longer. Singer continues to explain that, *"The more you are willing to just let the world be something you are aware of, the more it will let you be who you are, the awareness, the self, the Altman, the Soul. You realize you are not who you thought you were. You're not even a human being. You just happen to be watching one"* [yourself]. You are a spirit soul experiencing a human body. As his analysis deepens on the question of "Who am I," he suggests that, *"one ask the question ceaselessly, constantly. Ask it and you will notice that you are the answer. There is no intellectual answer... you are the answer. Be the answer, and everything will change."*

Decide to be spiritual. Decide to grow spiritually. Without a decision to move forward, you will stay where you are. John Holland (2018) reminds us that, *"Once you learn to lead a more spiritually enriched life, you'll be able to access all the unlimited resources that are available to each and every one of us. Once you begin to recognize that, you'll start to feel, see, and experience a world that you never thought possible."*

Sometimes we just don't understand why something is happening to us, but if we calm ourselves and look to God for answers, it all becomes clear that it is intended to lead us to a blessing as stated in this poem by my grandson as he dealt with a lifelong health issue.

Plans for You

What the hell did God do to me?
I never asked for this to be.

Why did God choose me?
Did I do something so wrong for him to say
"You're the unlucky?"

When will God stop this pain we are going through,
because now it's just not me, it's two.

Where I was asking God was all the wrong places.
I needed to ask from my heart and not certain spaces.

Why? Asked again.

If patient and calm, I find why God blessed me for so long.
Richard N. Campbell

Spend some time and do the exercises following this chapter using your journal to write your answers to the questions that are designed to help you make this a part of your life. It will be important to be able to go back and re-read what you write today to see if you are still on the right track a few weeks from now.

There will be more clarity about what being spiritual really means as we cover the Elements of Spiritually and Elements of Love in future chapters.

Exercises for Chapter 2

1. Assess your position on Spirituality:
   - What does "being Spiritual" mean to you?
   - Do you want a more main-stream religion with a church body to worship with?
   - Do you want a more personal one-on-one with your God and your own spiritually?

   (You can have both at the same time or singularly. It is your choice.)

2. Assess your level of Spirituality: List what you believe.
   - How well do you know your God?
   - How well do you know what spirituality is?
   - What are you already doing that will make spirituality grow? (Meditation, Prayers, etc.)

3. Even if you have not yet decided, pretend you have decided that you want to use this blessed time to learn to grow spiritually.

   - List three things you can do to get you started. (For example: read books, learn to meditate, find friends or others that are spiritual and talk with them, learn more about the components of spirituality: love, compassion, harmony, forgiveness, etc.

4. Assess how well your feelings about yourself might cause you to not grow more spiritual right now.
   - What do you dislike about yourself?
   - What do you like about yourself?
   - What can you do differently to learn to love ALL things about yourself?

PART 2

Elements of Spirituality

Introduction to Part 2
Elements of Spirituality

    Breaking down Spirituality into smaller individual pieces helps us to understand what spirituality really is. It directs those who want to be more spiritual to identify where you are already strong, and where you may need to add more spiritual energy to your life. Focusing on these elements assists you in doing something positive while navigating through the emotionally wroth time frame of anticipatory grief.

3
Spiritual Self-Responsibility

*Your human nature was content to become more intelligent,
your Divine nature calls for more wisdom and truth.
...liberate yourselves from your lower natures.*

Maureen Moss

This chapter begins to explore the Elements of Spirituality. Later chapters will explore Elements of Love. When we focus on all the parts and how they fit together, we can learn how to become more spiritual and how to love more. We start with spiritual self-responsibility.

Who is responsible for what happens to us? Some religions teach that God is responsible for everything good that happens to us in our lives; that he is blessing us in this way. On the other hand, these same religions teach that everything bad that happens to us is by the power of the Devil, causing us to stray from the straight and narrow path instead of obeying God's wishes for our lives. Many people wonder why God allows bad things to happen, especially to good people. Then when something terrible does happen, society is ready to say that it probably is because we went against God's wishes for our lives. It is depicted as a form of God's punishment.

We must remember that God gave us free choice. If we choose to not follow God's teachings and choose to live in a way that is less than we planned, God will still love us and will not punish us for these decisions. God knows that whatever experiences we do have will teach us lessons. It may not be the lesson that we planned, but we will still know better what worked and what didn't and be better able to make a different decision next time we are confronted with the same circumstances. God gave us free choice; why would he be angry or upset if we used it?

God continues to send the stream of well-being in hopes that we will decide to raise our spiritual energy to a point that we will receive the blessings that he is sending our way. In cases of extreme danger, of course God and his Angels are able and do send these streams of well-being directly to us no matter what level we are at, no matter how low we have become in our existence. God is love. God is all powerful and He could just force us to follow our (God's and your) plan. But we would be robots and not really growing spiritually in the way that moves us to a more glorious place. We would not know God and his love for us as the poem, "Wait," in Chapter One has so elegantly stated.

When thinking spiritual self-responsibility, we do not need to believe that if we do something in life that we or society perceive as wrong or bad, that it happened because the Devil made us do it and now God will punish us. This is truly a negative way to look at life and actually holds us back from spiritual development. Break the shackles of the idea that the Devil is controlling you. Take responsibility for your actions and "right" them. Remember these truths, God is always with you; God doesn't judge you. God only loves you. God gave you free choice. It is okay to use it. This is where spiritual self-responsibility comes into play.

Whether you are good or bad in society's eyes, God loves you regardless. God is always sending you love and blessings. If we feel we are not receiving them it is not God turning away from us; it is us, as individuals, that have lowered our spiritual energy vibration to the point that we are not able to receive the blessings that God is sending to us. But God continues to send the blessings anyway. Take responsibility to lift yourself (your spiritual energy), through prayer (talking with God), meditation (listening to God), random acts of kindness and love for yourself and others in your life and your spiritual energy will rise to meet God's energy.

To look at it from a different standpoint, many believe that we each plan our life before we are conceived, while we are still souls in the spiritual realm. Our soul wants to continue to grow more spiritual and picks a human body and brain including parents and siblings that will be most likely to help us attain our goal of spiritual growth through experiences on Earth. God is well aware of these plans as He is present when we make these plans and He helps us to attain them. After all, he wants our souls to grow more spiritually, too. Along the way on our journey, we meet people (Souls) that will help us attain fulfilling our plan. God places them there, as well as events and situations that give us opportunities to make decisions, choices that move us along on our journey to our very own destiny.

We must take responsibility for our actions and not be blaming God for bad things. Perhaps in our original plan, we planned a devastating event because it would bring us closer to our goal of growing more spiritual. Perhaps we had in our plan that if something wasn't a certain way at a certain point in our life this devastating event would come into play. Because of it, we do grow more spiritual. If this were part of our belief system, we would see this event as a product of our own making and take self-responsibility for the occurrence of it and not blame God for doing something bad to us, punishing us. We would see it as ultimately becoming a blessing and an experience that boosted our spiritual growth.

Learn to live your life from your Soul's level of energy. Live from the "inside out." Your Soul is the same thing as your Higher Self. It lives inside your heart chakra. It is fed spiritual energy through the other chakras energy centers; the three chakras above the heart that act as pathways to the Divine Energy of God. (See my book, *Spiritual Reflections... I Tried, God Helped* for a short discussion of the subject of chakras.)

God is always sending Divine Energy. We just need to keep our connections with the spiritual realm and accept the blessings. It is true that God brings us to certain challenges so that we can grow spiritually. He knows our plan and He helps us by leading us to the appropriate events that we can use for ourselves to grow spiritually. When God puts these challenges in front of us, we can go into them head on and work our way out, while asking for Divine Assistance and knowing that God knows our plan and is helping us attain it. Or we can go into it without regard for the spiritual teachings and blessings that we could have and suffer longer for making that decision. It is our free choice; it is not God punishing us as society would like us to think.

We have free choice and either choice will bring us information and help us grow by learning lessons. Nothing comes into our lives that is not meant for our good. Our society side doesn't see things the same as the spiritual side does. If we allow ourselves to get mired down in society's way to explain things instead of accepting that this thing that society says is so bad for us is really there for our ultimate good, we could be missing out on wonderful blessings from God.

This happens during anticipatory grieving, as well. This long, time frame is there for our spiritual growth. Accept it and grow from it. See it as a blessing in countless ways. It will make life easier, and you will be happier than if you sulked and whined over your situation at this time in your life.

Take responsibility for your own path, your spiritual journey, and grow closer to God. Listen to your Higher Self which is the God within. Live from the inside. Think, listen, see the difference of earth's societal way and God's spiritual way. Life will be so much happier as you grow more spiritual. Take responsibility for yourself, stop blaming the Devil and/or God for what is happening to you. See this awful thing, anticipatory grief, as a pathway to more spiritual growth. Look for the good in a bad situation. It is always there. It is there for your ultimate good and spiritual growth. It is the silver lining of our life on Earth.

For those of you that find yourself in the anticipatory grieving situation and like the idea of using this time to grow more spiritual, but do not hold to the teachings of Christianity, you can look at these teachings on a metaphysical level and see that God had more in mind than just the physical life of Jesus. Jesus was sent by God to teach us about His love. When we focus on love there is much to learn from the crucifixion and resurrection of Jesus.

Marianne Williamson (2004) has this to say on this subject, *"The crucifixion is not specifically a Christian concept, metaphysically, it is a pattern of energy, demonstrated physically in the life of Jesus but experienced metaphysically in the life of everyone. Energetically, it symbolizes a pattern of thought. Death is its mission and life is its enemy, for it is the mind at work against God. Thus, the drama of every human life, is as love is born into the world and then it is crucified by fear."*

"...Resurrection, like crucifixion, is a metaphysical truth; It is God's response to the ego, or the ultimate triumph of love. All that is ever going on, in any situation, is when love appears, it is crucified, but ultimately love holds sway. There is a dark force, not outside us but within us, always at work to destroy the love that God creates. That force, or ego, is held in play by our belief that we are separate from God and from each other; it expresses itself constantly through judgement and balance. It is every unkind word, attack, thought, or violent action. It is always active, as long as it has fear to feed it."

"The resurrection is God's answer to the crucifixion; it is His uplifting of our consciousness to the point where the effects of fear are cancelled. Our holiness, God's love within us, is the only way humankind has ever transcended darkness, and it is the only way we ever will."

Therefore, if you want to travel this path of growing more spiritual, take responsibility for yourself and your path. We must focus on love, God's love, and increase it in our own hearts. It doesn't matter what religion you are or are not, you can enhance your current belief system without ever changing your current religious affiliations. Just live and grow in God's love and you will live a happier life, not only while here on earth, but you will have helped your Soul elevate in sacred energy for when you go back home to the other side.

This is a poem that expresses "life" by one of God's finest, my grandson, Rick Campbell.

Life

Some people think life is a game,
Some people think life is a shame.

I believe life is a blessing,
I believe life is a lesson.

When you believe, look at all you achieved,
When you believe, look at all you have received.

Richard N. Campbell

Go to your journal and do the exercises for this chapter. The questions are designed to help you spend time analyzing your spiritual responsibility as it is now and how it could change. Please try to answer each question and please write your thoughts down so you can go back at a later date and re-read them again and again. You will see changes over time.

Exercises for Chapter 3

1. Do you want to be more spiritual?
   - List how growing spiritually might help you to get through this period of anticipatory grieving.
   - How can it help you with other relationships as well as your loved one that is dying?

2. Do you take Spiritual Responsibility for yourself?
   - List the ways you always take spiritual responsibility for yourself.

3. Do you want to be more Spiritually Responsible?
   - List the ways you could improve for the future to take more Spiritual Responsibility now. For example: Just consider what if you did develop a plan for yourself to learn and improve in certain behaviors (compassion, forgiveness, benevolence, and mercy) and the possibility that what happens in your life is because you planned it to happen so you could improve. Wouldn't you have to practice in order to be good at it, to see improvement?
   - List ways that changing how you look at tragic events in your life could help you to grow spiritually and be happier as you see the good, the silver lining, in the awful events. (Because they are there!)

4. List the ways that you respect and love God.

4
EGO

Wisdom is knowing I am nothing,
Love is knowing I am everything, and
Between the two my life moves.
                    Nisargadatte Maharaj

The ego is part of our human life. It can help us get to where we want to be in life, or it can be an obstacle that leads us in the wrong direction. The idea is to master the ego so we can get all the "good" from it and discard or override the ego to allow guidance from God to come through and direct our actions and thoughts. Some think of the ego as the true Devil rather than the Devil being a separate entity. None-the-less, the ego is an Element of Spirituality because we must master it in order to grow.

Maureen Moss (2004) explains it this way. *"For anyone not sure of what the ego is, it's the part of the mind that believes in division. It's usually judging, perceiving, creating highs and lows based on something external, or coming up with conflicts that symbolize separation."*

It is the voice in our head that tells us what to do, say or how to act. It is the voice that wants us to believe that we are in control of everything in our life, that we are the best person for a task, or the top person in the room. Or it can tell us that we are "no good." The ego gets in the way most of the time because it is noisy, self-serving and clamoring for attention constantly saying, "Look at me!"

Eckhart Tolle (2003), tells us that, "*The ego needs to be in conflict with something or someone. That explains why you are looking for peace and joy and love but cannot tolerate them for very long. You say you want happiness but are addicted to your unhappiness. Your unhappiness ultimately arises not from the circumstances of your life, but from the conditioning of your mind.*"

Being aware of this activity in the mind and separating out the duality of the earth-bound human mind, we can see the difference. When we are working from the God mind (our Soul), we know peace and unity as the God mind knows nothing but peace, unity, and love. The ego loves to foster separation between mortal mind and God mind. Maureen Moss (2002) gives us an acronym for EGO. It is *"Edging God Out." With the ego running things, deep soul connection, and therefore true happiness is not possible."*

If you are blaming God for something in your life that is causing you pain and suffering... STOP! All pain and suffering arise solely from the ego and not from God. You are blaming God for what you have allowed your ego to do to you.

Tolle again explains that, "*Almost every ego contains at least an element of what we might call "victim identity." Some people have such strong victim image of themselves that it becomes the central core of their ego. Resentment and grievances form an essential part of their sense of life.*" He continues to say to those that are doing this, "*... you have constructed an identity for yourself that is much like a prison whose bars are made of thought forms. See what you are doing to yourself. Feel the emotional attachment you have to your victim story and become aware of the compulsion to think or talk about it. Complaining and reactivity are favorite mind patterns *through which the ego strengthens itself. As long as the ego runs your life, most of your thoughts, emotions, and actions arise from desire and fear."*

Think of your life as a movie with two directors.
1) Ego: One director is making a movie about fears, anger, scarcity, anxiety and hate.
2) Holy Spirit: The other director is a movie about love, peace, abundance and happiness.

Our goal is to become aware of the director from which we are taking orders. Eckhart Tolle (2005) also says that, *"Whenever you are in a negative state, there is something in you that wants the negativity, that perceives it as pleasurable, or you would not hang onto negativity, make yourself and others miserable and create disease in your body. When there is negativity in you, if you can become aware at the moment that there is something in you that takes pleasure in it or believes it has a useful purpose, then you are becoming aware of the ego directly. The moment this happens your identity has shifted from ego to awareness. This means the ego is shrinking and awareness is growing."* Peace, after all is the end of ego for this situation. Learn to analyze each negative situation to see which director's orders you are following.

Marianne Williamson (2004) has this to say about the ego. *"When the ego steps back, the power of God can step forward. It is the moment of quiet, the Holy Instant, when the spirit enters and makes right all things. We are so much more powerful when surrounded by silence. Taking a deep breath, knowing that what you don't say can be as powerful as what you do say, thinking deeply about something before making a response... such actions leave room for the spirit to flow, to harmonize your circumstances and move them in a more positive direction. God's Spirit will always reveal the truth to us if we simply don't block His guidance. The ego is working hard to make* us believe that our decisions makes us special. That we don't need anyone to help us run our life."

Colin Tipping (2002) shares his thoughts on this matter of ego. *"The idea that our decisions matter in the overall scheme of things is just our ego trying to make us feel separate and special. The Universe has everything handled no matter what we decide. But how we make those decisions... whether from love or fear, greed or generosity, false pride or humility, dishonesty or integrity matters to us personally because each decision we make affects our vibration."*

This spiritual energy "vibration" Tipping discusses affects how well we can receive God's messages and his grace into our lives. God loves us no matter what we say or do. God is always sending us love, even when we think we do not deserve it. Believing we do not deserve it or more importantly that we do not need it, causes us to have a lower spiritual vibration. The lower vibration blocks us from receiving from the universe.

To raise your spiritual vibration, simply close your eyes and grow quiet in your mind. Think of God's love for you and your love for God. Do this for as long as you can, at least for five minutes or longer, if possible. Having your mind quiet turns off the ego and allows a connection with God to strengthen. This process is a simple process called meditation. Yes, it is that simple.

As you get quiet and go within, you will learn to "know" God. Practice meditating routinely and you will not only learn to know God, but yourself as well. It takes practice, but in time, as you continue the process of meditation, you will begin to experience a shift. Let it ebb and flow instead of trying to control it. Turn off the ego.

Moss (2002) describes it this way, *"You will be aware of the intensification of an experience and then its dissolving into nothingness leaving behind a trailing wake of self-discovery. In the privacy of your own inner space, you will begin to have an intimate relationship with your inner space, you will have an intimate relationship with your true self, your soul and God."* In turn, you will grow in wisdom.

I recently had an occasion to see and experience this "Ego Trip" up close and personal. I asked someone, who's skills I highly value, to edit a portion of this project. She did and then sent it back to me via an email attachment. When I saw the attachment and knew it was ready for me to read, my ego jumped into action. It said to me, "Do you want to give someone else credit for your work? You are smart, you can write it well yourself. You don't need her." I felt agitated and angry. I suddenly stopped said to myself, "WHAT is going on here?"

I realized it was my ego feeding me these thoughts. I decided to pray and meditate about the edited portion before I read it. During meditation, Spirit (God) said to me, "Even Dr. Wayne Dyer had someone read and help edit his stuff." Since I admire Dr. Wayne Dyer's writings, I could see that my ego was working overtime here, and I decided to read the edited portion while not letting my ego get in the way. I turned off my ego! My, Oh My! She had done a beautiful job editing it. I loved it! When I shared my experience with her, she said she didn't edit it alone... God had helped her edit it. No wonder it was done so well!

Remember that knowledge comes from the outside in, wisdom moves from the inside out. Learn to live your life from the inside, from your soul level.

Remind yourself to analyze things from the point of view of the Spiritual Realm and not the point of view that our society pushes us to use.

Dr. Wayne Dyer (2007) had a special perspective on the ego, saying *"Do a mind exercise that will put you in touch with the Peace of the Tao."* Tao is short for Tao Te Ching, which is a book of wisdom written 500 years before Jesus came to earth. It means "The Great Way" and is balanced, moral, spiritual, and always concerned with working for the good of all. He asks us to say, *"It is all perfect. God's love is everywhere and forgets no one. I trust in His force to guide me, and I am not allowing ego to enter now. Notice how free you feel when you relax into this no fears, no worries attitude."*

Again, Marianne Williamson (2004) leaves us with this thought:

"Ego says: Once everything falls into place, I will find peace.

Spirit says: Once I find peace, everything falls into place."

To make this information part of your personal life, do the exercises at the end of this chapter.

Exercises for Chapter 4

1. Think of a time when you realized that your ego had gotten in the way of you being successful.
   - Did anyone get hurt emotionally because your ego was working overtime?
   - Did you get hurt emotionally?
   - Do you now realize that you were following the wrong Movie Director?

2. Think of a time that you realized that you were purposely pushing your ego to the background and made the decision to follow the Holy Spirit as your Movie Director. Did you have greater success?

3. Practice turning off your ego. Write down what you can say to yourself to make this happen.

4. Practice, Practice, Practice!

5
Time

*When you are willing to honor Divine Order,
you will Learn how to be flexible.
Bend your way,
asking the Divine Forces to show you the way.*

*Done
D = Divine
O = Order
N = Now
E = Expressing
Iyanla Vanzant*

Some might think it odd that time could be referred to as an Element of Spirituality. It is an element because time in the spiritual realm is different than earth time. We must know the difference and take it into account when we ask for something to happen through prayer, meditation, or manifesting.

Time on Earth is different than time in the spiritual realm because on Earth, time is linear. We think of time as being fast or slow. It is divided into past, present, or future. But in the spiritual realm everything happens in the "now." That is a hard concept to understand. What may seem like an eternity or at least a very long time here on earth, say ten years just for an example, is nothing more than a blink of an eye where we are going someday when we die.

When we pray, we expect the prayer to be answered in the affirmative. It is as though we expect what we ask for to be here today, now, or at least sooner rather than later. But God and His universe (all of God's helpers, i.e., Angels, Guides, Teachers and Masters) are going to answer the prayer in a way that is best for our highest good and the highest good for all concerned with the prayer request. The timing might be wrong for us to have it when we want it because other pieces might not be in place yet. So, when we pray, we must keep this in mind and allow for Divine timing to be just right for all concerned.

An example comes to mind to demonstrate how this works. My husband, Norm, and I wanted to sell our two RV lots in Arizona after we quit going there as snowbirds. I prayed for them to sell right away, like in the next few months. We had sold a third lot with the house on it within two weeks of making the decision to sell. We felt so blessed and the buyers also felt blessed. The timing was right, because it was Divine timing and right for both parties—plus the housing market was right as well. Selling the remaining two lots did not fall into place so quickly and easily.

I used manifesting methods along with prayer. I realized that when the prayer's answer was "No, not yet," and when the manifesting didn't manifest as I thought it should, then I knew I must be patient and wait for Divine timing. My prayer request was answered, but the answer was, "Wait."

One lot sold six years after I had first asked for it to sell; the other lot sold eleven months thereafter. When the first RV lot sold, it felt like a miracle. I received a phone call asking what the price was. The man said I will give you $2,000 less than that in cash and I want it to close escrow in one month. Since I was in Idaho and he was in Arizona, where the lot was, he went to the title company and started the process. All went well and it closed a few days early. I know the second lot will go just as smoothly when the timing is right for all concerned.

In the meantime, and because we had to wait, I learned a lot and am grateful for the experiences I had. I learned how to be a good landlord while renting the lots out to other snowbirds with their RVs. I met several good people as renters along the way. I even had to say good-bye to one renter as she passed away while she and her husband were renting from us. I had the blessed opportunity to be supportive to the husband afterwards.

When it appears like our prayers are being ignored, we must remember, trust and believe that the timing is just not right for it all to come together for our better good and the better good for all involved. It is an opportunity to practice patience.

Marianne Williamson (2004) helps us to understand the biblical terms pertaining to time.

- *"Time shall be no more"* means the end of the illusion of linear time and beginning of an eternal ***now***.
- *"Everlasting"* means *"always there,"* not an eternal reality that begins when this life is over, and some other life begins. It refers to a moment by moment reality that has gone on forever, is true this instant, and will endure forever.
- *"Eternity"* means never-ending presence in which God is." It is the dimension of His power, and to the extent that we use the present to focus on past or future, we dis-empower ourselves.

She points out that the tennis player doesn't have time to think about the ball they just missed because it would take away from the effort to hit the next ball. We should take notice of this analogy and how it works in our life not just during a tennis game. Some things are just not worth giving our attention to as there are more important things ahead that need your attention.

How important is a single second of our time? A single second can make a difference in our lives or the life of another. A miracle can happen. In that "Holy Instant" you can change your mind. You can know you will live your life differently for the rest of your life. You can change your life by changing your mind, your thoughts. Deciding to live a more spiritual life is the best thing you can do for your physical self and of course, your spiritual self. Living from the inside out brings more joy, wisdom and harmony to you and your loved one.

Growing more spiritual is not always easy as it may require some major changes in your everyday decisions and behaviors along with a lot of practice. A good way to begin is to pay attention to how you react to everyday situations. Your "go to" reaction may be shown as anger or other behaviors that may hurt you or someone else. In time, "react" can be changed to "respond." Respond is a learned response. Learning more about how to live a spiritual life means learning how to have a "learned loving response" to situations that used to cause an anger reaction. Earthly time will allow this growing spiritual experience to happen.

When you are in a situation where you are experiencing anticipatory grief, especially when dealing with your loved one as a caregiver, but also in other roles as well, you will be given many opportunities to change your angry or unkind reactions to loving responses. This is why anticipatory grieving is such a blessing. You have time to practice changing the way you respond to your love one before they pass, and the new behavior spills over to other relationships as well.

During this period, time seems to go slowly, especially as the pages of the calendar turn and the seasons pass by. It seems like endless tomorrows are before you to remain in this situation of waiting for your loved one to die. Many emotions are experienced—some good, many are bad. That is until you open your heart and allow God to take control, instead of your ego. In time, you are able to understand that your wanting this situation to be over is just a natural human happening. The guilt that you experience over having those emotions and thoughts just makes you human. Remember to say, (and mean it) "I don't mind what happens." When you stop trying to control everything, life gets better.

When you make the decision to be more spiritual in your "go to" reaction, and you want it to be based on love rather than anger or bullying, you will have so much help from the heavens to continue to do this for yourself and your loved one. Often the response can be just saying nothing and let it be. Each time you do not react in an angry manner, you grow in compassion as you "upgrade" your reaction to a learned response. In doing so, your Soul has grown more spiritual as it has moved to a higher spiritual vibration, as well. In the past, you may have hurt their feelings, whereby now they feel loved. It all comes together through Divine timing.

When you have something to focus on besides your grief—like improving yourself, changing your reactions into loving responses, showing the love that you do have for your loved one, and focusing on the now in your life—this extended period of time turns into something wonderful after all. When your loved one does finally die, you will rejoice that you did the very best you could to care for them and show them your love, even if it wasn't returned. If you think of growing spiritually as the basis for how to make this time better and you practice, practice, practice, then you will have also grown spiritually. This will contribute to your state of happiness for the rest of your life in all of your other relationships. Over time, harmony rules when you use love!

Now do the exercises at the end of this chapter. Write your thoughts in your journal.

Exercises for Chapter 5

1. Make a short list of happenings in your life where the timing was just right, and all pieces of the puzzle fell into place just right. Can you see where God had a hand in this timing?

2. Think of a time when you lost your temper and verbally lashed out at someone. Did any good come from it?

3. How could it have been more pleasant for all if you had used love instead?

4. Forgive yourself and resolve to learn to handle these situations differently in the future. How will you do this?

6
When to Die

*Every death is an extremely joyful birth
into a higher dimension of awareness and being.*
Doreen Virtue and James Van Praagh

Nothing could be closer to an Element of Spirituality than dying. Since we will all experience dying and entering the true Heavenly Realm someday, knowing more about dying will make the occurrence less frightening.

There is no pain in death. Doreen Virtue and James Van Praagh (2013) tells us that, *"As humans we must begin to understand that death itself is not to be feared. The transition when a soul actually leaves the physical vessel is indeed painless. This has been proved via countless near-death exercises. There is an immediate sense of being free. The soul no longer experiences the physical discomforts that he or she had lived with towards the end."*

Modern society would have us believe that death is an anomaly, the most dreadful event that could ever happen. But in actuality, death is the most normal thing that could ever happen to us. Death is inseparable from and just as natural as its polarity, birth. Eckhart Tolle (2003), tells us that, *"Death is not the opposite of life. Life has no opposite. The opposite of death is birth. Life is eternal. There is still a widespread denial of death in Western Cultures. Even old people try not to speak or think about it. A culture that denies death inevitably becomes shallow and superficial, concerned only with external form of things. When death is denied, life loses its depth."*

No one dies *when* they are not supposed to or *how* they are not supposed to. When a person dies, their Soul has finished all that they wanted to do, or they would not have died. When we plan our life before we are born, along with all the details of what we want to accomplish in our life, we also have planned when we will leave and how we leave. Think about the fact that most of those who have gone through a near-death experience lost their fear of death. What does this tell you? It tells me that death itself is not a scary thing.

Those are bold statements, but since we are talking about grieving for someone dying, it seems appropriate to talk about death for a few minutes. Think about how you have viewed the death of someone that was murdered. Society tells us that this is terrible. We must now punish someone for the act that caused this death. We may even go so far as to put another person (the murderer) to death as well.

Yes, we must have law and order in our civilized culture or society. But *if* we come from a belief that we are spiritual souls that came to earth to experience a human body, we can view all deaths differently than what society now tells us. If we can also accept and believe that we plan, before birth, what our experiences will be while here, we can look deeper at the events that led up to the murdering of that person which enables its soul to return to its heavenly home.

That soul likely had a plan to experience dying by being murdered. (Another bold statement by societies' standards.) Perhaps that murdered person had been a murderer in a previous life and karma was being played out, or that soul just wanted to add that experience to their soul's list of wanted experiences.

In this scenario, many emotions come into play that the person (that Soul) may have wanted to experience while they are here on Earth. For every accident or death, there is potentially a redemptive dimension of which we are unaware.

You may ask why anyone would want that experience. Experiencing those emotions brings our soul to a level of greater spiritual vibration and thus greater spiritual growth. Perhaps it is karma as suggested above. Perhaps not. While we are souls on the other side, nothing seems bad because we are in a state of bliss, with love all around us. We think we can do anything, that you can go through anything while here on Earth. It is our school away from home. We will never experience bad things in Heaven. We can learn, but learning is much slower because we can't really experience some of the dark side that is available on Earth.

Please, be assured that the soul had finished all that they wanted to experience. Otherwise they would not have died. If you don't believe in reincarnation, this theory will not appeal to you. It is not important for you to believe in reincarnation to grow spiritually, it just gives meaningful answers to so many questions that we have as humans. Reincarnation gives us opportunities to rethink all that happens to us and gives us answers to questions such as why babies and young adults die, or why good people have bad things happen to them.

Ultimately, the death of a physical body is a decision made by the soul of that physical body after their life plans have been fulfilled. God comes into play here also. If we are not supposed to die, God won't let it happen. On the other hand, God may give us several calls to come home to Heaven, leaving it up to us to choose to stay or go. But when a person does die, be assured that all that that soul needed to gain during their life here on Earth has been gained.

It is not scary to them at the point of death. Most people become deeply peaceful and almost luminous just before they die, as if something is shining through their eyes and all around them. There is no psychological suffering left. The mind-made ego called "me" has already surrendered. They are at peace as their soul realizes that they have experienced all that they wanted to experience by coming to earth and now they want to go back to their heavenly home. It was reported by the media that when Steve Jobs of Apple Computers was in the process of passing away, his sister reported that the last thing he said was, "WOW!" He apparently was seeing something simply wonderful and it says volumes to me about the beauty and peace that awaits us all.

I want to share a personal example with you. My own daughter, Kathy, died when she was four years old. I believe that her soul was highly elevated. She was born with Down's Syndrome in 1963 but functioned as a high-level special needs child. Because of her affliction, I started working at a hospital for the mentally ill and/or impaired when she was two years old. Her coming into my life led me to want to know more about her condition, therefore I entered the field of nursing, which turned out to be my life's work. I love being a Registered Nurse. It was what I was supposed to do with my life. Later it was revealed to me that she and I had made a deal (a contract between souls) during the time while planning our lives for this incarnation. She agreed to come and be my daughter, but she said she didn't want to stay long. She would stay only as long as it took to get me on my right path, in other words, God's and my intended spiritual path.

While still a soul of light in the spiritual realm, I wanted to have opportunities to grow in compassion and I wanted to be a nurse in this lifetime in order to grow spiritually. When Kathy's soul saw that I was firmly on my way and on my correct path, her soul decided to go back to our heavenly home as she intended. She is still with me in spirit from time to time. April 6, 2019 marked 52 years since she passed. I still miss her physical presence and love her with all my heart. But knowing it was her plan to not stay long has helped me to move forward on my path, which is to share God's light by sharing personal spiritual experiences like this with you.

Virtue and Van Praagh (2013) remind us that, *"Death is very much an illusion. A soul can never be harmed, and nothing can put out the light of your being. There is no condemnation when you cross over, just an awareness of the choices your soul needed to experience. When a soul goes home and is freed from limitations of the earthly mind, it will be restored to the fullest of its glory and continue to live in the eternal energy of God."*

Teresa Caputo (2015), the Long Island Medium, gives her thoughts on the question of when people die in events like September 11, 2001, did they choose to die then and in that way? *"What Spirit does tell me happens is that with say, 9/11's first responder's souls, they knew they'd pass away doing a civic duty, or with soldiers, that they'd die serving their country... all during a block of time called their "destiny." All their souls knew, (1) They would die in an allotted window while, (2) pursuing lessons that impacted their soul's growth and others on, (3) their souls generally charted path from God."*

Linda Howe (2016) continues the discussion, *"We do not know when we will die. We only know that it will happen at the perfect time, God's Divine time. Given that thought, it is best to acknowledge and accept that everything in your life, whether you like it or not, is there for you, for your growth, for your good, that nothing can enter your life unless it is ultimately good for you. That includes when you die and how you die. It has the potential to aid you in knowing your own essential worth, that of others, and of life itself."*

Robert Schwartz (2012) also has some thoughts on this subject of when and how we die, especially regarding pre-birth planning of large-scale "negative" events. For example, take the tsunami that hit South East Asia a few years ago. One hundred thousand (100,000) people were killed. He explains that it is his understanding that, *"Those souls hoped before they were born that the Earth would be at a certain vibration by a certain point in linear time. These souls agreed before birth that if it looked as though the Earth were not going to get there, they would give their lives in a large-scale, natural disaster, because they knew that the result would be a worldwide outpouring of love and compassion that would raise the Earth's vibration to the desired frequency. You may recall that this is exactly what happened. The governments of the world put aside their differences and cooperated to funnel aid to South East Asia. This outpouring of love and compassion raised the frequency of our planet to the level those souls had intended."*

He goes on to remind us that, *"You've probably heard the expression, "Where you stand depends upon where you sit." The tsunami is a great example of that expression. If you are a human who "sits" in the third dimension,* [the dimension we live in here on Earth] *then your likely "stand" on the tsunami is that it was a terrible tragedy. If, however, you are a spirit guide* [or a passed on loved one] *who "sits" in the fourth dimension* [Heaven's Spiritual Realm] *then where you likely "stand" on the tsunami is that it was a great blessing to our world. Two diametrically opposed viewpoints, both of which are correct from the perspective of the observer. As you look at the challenge in your own life, see if you can shift from the perspective of the personality* [Third Dimension] *to that of your soul* [Forth Dimension]. *You will see your life in an entirely new light".*

When we look at anticipatory grief from this perspective, we see that the long, linear time frame that it takes some persons to die is actually a gift and a blessing. So much can be accomplished during this precious time. Couples can grow closer through the knowledge that time is short, no matter how long it takes. Love can grow even more now. It becomes a time for a focus on spiritual growth in one or both persons or even more if you include all of those that love and care about the person that is dying. Opportunities abound for growth in compassion, harmony, grace, gratitude, wisdom, forgiveness, patience and courage. The list is almost endless. We can truly use this time to grow spiritually when we view life from our soul's perspective instead of from the human personality that is caught up in what society tells us to think.

Eckhart Tolle (2005) reminds us, *"This too shall pass."* This goes well with the situation of anticipatory grieving. He goes so far as to tell us to have "This too shall pass," engraved on a ring. *"The ring serves to remind us of the fact of impermanence which, when recognized leads to non-attachment. Non-attachment, non-resistance, non-judgement are the three aspects of true freedom and enlightened living."* Tolle's words have a deeper purpose and that is, *"to make you aware of the fleetingness of every situation, which is due to the transience of all forms, good or bad. When you become aware of the transience of all forms, your attachment to them lessens and you dis-identify from them to some extent. Being detached does not mean that you cannot enjoy the good that the world has to offer. In fact, you can enjoy it more."*

"This too shall pass" brings detachment and with detachment another dimension comes into your life... "inner space." Through detachment, as well as non-judgement and inner non-resistance, you gain access to that dimension. It becomes as a stillness, a subtle peace deep within you, even in the face of something seemingly bad. There is space around the event."

You can focus more on the space of the event and less on the negatives. This is the awareness that the event is transitory and will someday pass. This is the peace of God. It brings you peace as you go through the trials of anticipatory grief. As you are growing into awareness at a rate that is respectful, kind, and manageable, anticipatory grief is allowing the time for you and your loved one to grow spiritually.

It allows you to grow more independent and figure things out in a calmer manner than a sudden death would allow. You get more time to say "good-bye," more time to grow deeper in love with each other. This will help you after your loved one is gone, as well as right now at this present moment. If you are the one that is facing death through an illness, this still has all the same meanings for you as well as your loved one.

We know that during the anticipatory grief period sometimes the patient has a sudden healing take place or at least there is a period of time whereby the symptoms are showing signs of not getting worse. Caroline Myss (1997) tells us that *"when illness is part of your journey, no medical intervention can heal you until your spirit has begun to make the changes that the illness was designed to inspire. The most healing option, when you are facing an illness as a spiritual challenge, is to rely on your spiritual practice to bring you the insights you need. Your practice can be a means of enduring the disease and healing it, or it can prepare you for the release of your life [death], if that is the Divine will for you. You need to redirect your faith from the physical realm to the spiritual realm."*

During anticipatory grief there is time to do this if you recognize that there is something positive you can do with this time. Again, see the time as a blessing for you and your loved one. Use this gift to grow spiritually by reading spiritual author's works. Develop a closer walk with God. Be open to change within yourself. Live life from the inside, your soul level and let the negatives of our society go. Drop all your negative thoughts into an imaginary river that is running in front of you. Let them go on down the river, flowing away from you, never to be seen again or to be worried about again. If the negative thoughts come back, you didn't toss ALL of the negativity into the imaginary river. This does take practice. It takes change of your physical behavior and change in your soul. Most of all it takes change in your thinking. Without change in your thinking, you will not be able to make changes in your behavior.

I have included another poem from my friend Linda Erickson. She wrote this poem after driving along a highway in Montana near the Sweet Grass Mountains. She was seeing death as a pleasant thing. It is a good reminder that our own death doesn't have to be a bad thing.

Going Home

When I am freed from old age
I shall soar with eagles
Above mountain snow fields
And feel clouds beneath my wings.

Or perhaps I will slip on silent paws
Into deep shadowed forests
To run with my pack
And serenade a full-bellied moon.

If it is the long sleep of winter
I'll dream in my den
Of swift waters, leaping trout,
And cubs tumbling in spring meadows.

When at last I am rested,
I shall run north with my herd
Through folded hills and greening valleys
All the way to those Sweet Grass Mountains.

Linda Lee Farrell Erickson - September 2011

While we are discussing the subject of dying, we should take a look at those that take their own life (suicide). Trudy Griswold, in her online newsletter for Angelspeake on June 11, 2018, shares with us what the Angels had to say about suicide. *"Some religious institutions teach that taking one's own life is never an option; and if you do choose this, the soul will not enter heaven. We angels say to you that this speculation is simply not true. When Trudy and Barbara wrote the book "Heaven and Beyond", we sent many stories of individuals who took their own lives telling that their soul was welcomed as they returned to heaven and how the loving angels helped escort their soul home to be with God and their loved one. Yes, child, there is no shame in making the extremely difficult decision to take one's life from our perspective. God has given each human the gift of free will while on Earth. Sometimes it is a choice that a person makes when life becomes too difficult and a soul becomes overwhelmed with the urge to return home to rest and begin another life cycle. Do not worry, we are always there with love."*

Some of you reading this book that do not believe in reincarnation will not appreciate this entry. But since this book is not derived from just one religious perspective, it has been included. As always, take what feels right for you and leave the rest. But for those of you that have lost a loved one due to suicide, you may find this entry comforting.

Go to your journal and have a conversation with yourself, record your thoughts and beliefs regarding death.

Exercises for Chapter 6

1. What are your thoughts on death?
   - Where will the dead go after death?

2. What are your beliefs on those that die young or a violent death?
   - Who is responsible?

3. Have you ever sat with a person as they were dying? Write about your experience.
   - What did you see?
   - What did you feel?

7
Fear

Even death is not to be feared
by one who has lived wisely.
Buddha

    Fear is an unpleasant emotion that we feel when we have an expectation, or an awareness of danger, or a threat that is likely to cause pain. It could be an awareness of impending evil, real or imagined. Anticipatory grieving is full of fear, if we let it be. Therefore, fear is listed as an Element of Spirituality for the sake of this book. Of course, we want to understand fear better so we can avoid it.

    When grieving has gone on for a long time, fear makes itself known in many ways. First, we fear living our lives without our loved one. After a while we fear that they won't die and we have to live out the rest of your life as a caregiver, restricted from doing the things we wanted to do while we are able, especially if we are already senior citizens. We fear large medical bills, care and upkeep of the home, even every day running of the household, like cooking and cleaning. When one is younger, they may fear the caring for and raising young children alone, forcing them to make decisions that they never had to make alone before.

    This brings us to the question, "Is life a journey or a destination?" Have you ever given any thought to that question? Pastor Tony L. Nelson, PhD (2017) shares his thoughts on this subject. He says, *"Your answer could ultimately determine your happiness and personal growth as a human being. If life is a destination, we have little occasion to believe that the purpose is more than protecting and maintaining our "space", creating a defensive approach to most of life."*

The defensive approach is full of fear, but Dr. Nelson continues to explain, *"If life is a journey, then we can embrace the constant challenges that bring change and experience significant growth as a result. Protecting our space leaves little room for creative thinking; while looking at life as a journey creates an attitude of abundance and curiosity."*

Either approach to life, journey or destination, is full of uncertainty. Eckhart Tolle (2005) tells us that *"If uncertainty is unacceptable to you, it turns into fear. But if uncertainty is perfectly acceptable it turns into increased aliveness, alertness, and creativity. Therefore, instead of just protecting your space you also want to learn to accept uncertainty on those constant challenges that bring change so you can experience significant spiritual growth while on your journey."*

Life's challenges bring us to the core of our soul's mission, which is always to help us raise awareness, release judgement, and create even more compassion for ourselves and others. To do this, it helps to first know our inner divinity. It works best when we release the outdated parent-child concept of our external God who operates on a reward and punishment system. Recognize that a Divine force is intrinsic to our every thought and action, that an inner force guides us to become ever more conscious.

Getting to know the nature of God who is within reveals your own innate power and allows you to become aware of how you co-create with God whatever you experience in your life, including your health. Fear interferes with the self-awareness of your power. When you base your choices on fear, chaos comes between you and your inner divinity. To decrease your susceptibility to fear, your spiritual life requires attention and nurturing. The human spirit requires daily nurturing through a spiritual practice such as prayer and/or meditation. These practices nourish the energy system and help unite mind, heart and spirit.

Bertrand Russell (1957) *told us that "fear is one of the main sources of cruelty. To conquer fear is the beginning of wisdom."* Allowing ourselves to fear is being cruel to ourselves. When we let those things dominate our thoughts and time, we do our selves a dis-service. Trusting that your God can lead you through this time in your life helps. Take time to get closer to your God. See this extended time of grief as a blessing as often as you can. Say to yourself, "So this is what is next God? Well okay, lead me through it."

Use this time to grow spiritually. It is good to have friends or acquaintances that you can talk to and learn from, but if you don't have that luxury you can still do it by starting or getting stronger in your own spiritual practices. If you are reading this book, then you are already interested in finding out what it means to grow spiritually. Focusing on spirituality gives you time to practice spiritual behaviors.

Love comes first. Love come last as well. With love all else falls into place. Love can be shown in many ways—compassion, forgiveness, benevolence, mercy, patience, service to others, and keeping harmony in all situations of your life. Love is even much more than these things. Love is all there really is. As you focus on love you grow spiritually. Start now to live your life from your soul level. Live life from the inside out. Live as though your humanness wasn't the most important thing to you. Focus on only what your soul tells you, not what your ego tells you. Push the ego aside and far, far to the background. The ego holds us back by feeding us information that makes us think we are in control of everything in our life. We are not!

So, my friend, set fear aside and be vaguely aware of the things that bring you fear. Put the ego far in the background and trust in God and the part of you that is God within. You will have fears come up from time to time, turn them over to God and continue down your path listening to your higher self, your spiritual self, your soul and move forward with love. This is especially important during the anticipatory grieving time. Most importantly, what you learn now will serve you well for the rest of your life.

Spend some time with your journal and write down your thoughts in this chapter's exercises.

Exercises for Chapter 7

1. Think of a time when you were fearful, angry and/or had a lot of anxiety. Note how you felt and why you felt so emotional.
   - Who was with you?
   - Did it help the situation?

2. Now think about a time when you were full of love, peace, and abundance. Note how you felt.
   - Was the same person with you?
   - Did it help the situation?

3. When either of these feelings, fear or peace, come up again in the future, explore which "director" you are taking orders from…. Your ego or God? (Remember the two Directors from chapter Four.)

4. Learn to explore and recognize whether your feelings represent hate or fear and what you can do differently in the future to bring your feelings to love and peace.

8
Relationships

Life is not a private affair.
A story and its lessons are only made useful if shared.
Dan Millman

    For the sake of discussion, consider relationships as an Element of Spirituality. As Dan Millman stated in the entry above, "life is not a private affair," therefore it is necessary to perceive relationships as a way to measure our progress in growing more spiritual. Relationships are key to finding the way to our own destiny.

    Hopefully the relationship with our loved one is truly a loving one. But sometimes, it just isn't. If you and your loved one are at odds with each other when anticipatory grieving begins, now is a good time to correct your thinking. *Your* thinking is focused on in this discussion because it is truly the only thing you can control. You can't control and are not responsible for how your loved one feels, thinks, believes or behaves. Eckhart Tolle (2003), points out that *"If her past were your past, her pain your pain, her level of consciousness your level of consciousness, you would think and act exactly as she does. With this realization comes forgiveness, compassion, peace."*

    Whether our relationship has always been good or often rocky, we can choose to look at the relationship in the best way for both ourselves and our loved one during this grieving period. Focus on love, come from the heart as you interact with others.

Sometimes the person dying is so overcome with sadness and anger, as they realize that they will be leaving this earthy plane, that they take their anger out on those closest to them. That may very well be you. There are some things you can do if you find yourself in this situation. First of all, love them. REALLY LOVE THEM! See them as their soul, not the physical person that you see in front of you. Their soul is beautiful, because it is pure love. It is their earthly physical brain and large ego that is acting out and causing you pain. Often their behavior will change to match your behavior. So, make your behaviors loving behaviors. Strive for harmony in every situation.

Robert Schwartz (2012) explains the actions of a loved one that is dying in this way... *"Often the challenge for the one needing care is to believe that they are worthy of such love. Feelings or belief of unworthiness are the primary reasons why we, as souls, plan pre-birth to need the care of another. We seek to discover while in body our inherent, limitlessness worth and so place ourselves in a position in which we require care so we may learn we are worthy of it. Like a candle in a dark room, our inner light may be most visible to us in the darkness of illness or incapacitation. When we come to know our infinite value, that is, when we feel it, then the caregiving may come to an end or it may continue as a form of service to the caregiver."*

He continues, *"What is in it for the caregiver? Caregivers may cultivate empathy and express love, often in ways they could not in previous lives. Opportunities and motivation to learn kindness, patience and compassion [abound]."*

Colin Tipping (2002) offers this explanation, likening it to attraction and resonance. *"Our spoken beliefs cause effects in our world. In addition, other people resonate with the energetic frequency of that belief. In other words, they vibrate sympathetically at the same rate with it. When they do so, they are attracted into our lives to mirror our beliefs back to us. That gives us a chance to look at, and if necessary, to change our minds about the belief. It is not only negative beliefs that get mirrored back to us, either. For example, if we are loving and trusting, we will tend to attract people into our lives who are likewise trustworthy and nurturing."*

It is not just about spoken beliefs, but actions also. This mirroring effect works many times during a relationship, and it is threatened by impending death, especially when the death is taking a very long time to happen. When you stay loving and you become nicer to the loved one that is causing you grief, what often happens, over time, is that the loved one starts mirroring you. Stated simply, when you start consistently being nicer, they become nicer too. I have experienced this myself as I have gone through my own anticipatory grieving for a loved one. It can be very rewarding as you see it unfold over time. Some think of it as karma. When you do good, good comes back to you.

Tipping continues, *"All relationships are for healing! We must understand this phenomenon and use Radical Forgiveness* [All is as it is supposed to be, therefore there is nothing to forgive.] *to stay in this relationship and fulfill its true spiritual purpose, which is to heal the people involved."* Use love during this time of grieving to strengthen your relationship with your loved one. Grow more spiritual yourself. As you grow closer to God, you outgrow your ego. The hope is, of course, that your loved one will grow more spiritual too.

Will you always be able to show love and control your ego during your anticipatory grieving time? No. You are human as you live in your physical body. But you can recognize when you didn't control your ego and make amends with yourself and your loved one, then move forward again to be successful in this endeavor next time. Your soul will grow too. God loves you through it all, no matter what the outcome.

Practicing this now and seeing the relationship improve through love, will make the time after death so much better. As you look back after their death and see that you did all you could for your relationship with your loved one, you will feel peace. This is true also for yourself as you go forward working through the grief that is almost certain to be there, even though you have been working through your grief for some time. You will be able to feel good about your efforts, having no regrets, only love for them and yourself.

As we have just discussed, your love can grow, even if you have a contentious relationship with your loved one that is dying. As you grow in how to show your love the patient grows too, that is if they don't have dementia. If some form of dementia is present, then you can still grow anyway and know you will have no regrets after the death has occurred. Sherrie Dillard (2013), shares her thoughts, *"The soul knows what it is doing. Trust that there is a likely meaningful soulful activity going on within your loved one who is unresponsive or sitting days upon days looking out the window. Even though an individual's behavior may appear to be strange and eccentric, the soul is attracting the conditions for its evolution and healing. The soul may be completing karma, releasing repressed energy, and revisiting choices and decisions. Entering into the spiritual realm as unencumbered and free as possible from unfinished business allows the soul to ascend into higher vibrations of blissful cosmic love."*

Occasionally there is a couple where both have dementia. This is certain to be a shared journey for this relationship, but the obvious lessons are likely for others, like family members that are close to this couple. The souls of all involved are exposed to special added spiritual growth opportunities. We currently have a situation like this in our family and it is easy to see for whom the lessons are meant to touch.

Sometimes the dying person denies that their life is waning and tries to do everything just as they always have. This decision makes things difficult for the family as the person doesn't accept his reduced ability. It keeps the family from moving on and preparing for the impending death. It is still important to approach this with love. So rather than push hard to get the dying loved one to see and accept where they are on their journey... use love to keep harmony. It is best to use the thought (to yourself), "I do not mind what he/she does" and really mean it. Although hard at first, because our ego wants to control the situation and society tells us that what they are doing should be addressed, we must push our ego down and focus on love and harmony. Remember that society is not always right. It is best to focus on spiritual ways to get through tough situations. Using the thought, "This too shall pass," will keep harmony. The death will happen in Divine time.

When you are the caregiver there are special circumstances that give you opportunities to experience important earth school lessons. This is planned long before you came into this life. You can look at it as something God planned for you, or you planned it for yourself or you and God planned it together. Choose which feels best for you and closest to your truth. None the less, this is part of your journey leading to your destiny. Your Soul has been given the opportunity to practice the lessons of unconditional love, compassion and selflessness. These things encompass the full scope of love. Although throughout all of this, you may feel too much is being demanded of you and your patience is being tested beyond strained limits. Your relationship may be strained as well. Often the dying person has become hard to live with, becoming selfish and stubborn, or especially insensitive to your needs thinking only of themselves. Love them anyway and focus on their souls, which are pure love.

Remember these loved ones and you are sharing soul lessons. This includes those with ALS, dementia, and unresponsiveness, which was just discussed. So much can be learned spiritually from being the caregiver. Each time you keep your anger from showing and treat the patient with kindness you and your soul grow in compassion. Learning how to do this can change your life, not only now but also on into the remainder of your life. It will help you improve all of your other relationships.

Allowing others to care for us (if we are the patient) can also be difficult when we are vulnerable, dependent, and at the mercy of others. It can be the ultimate test of our trust in others and God and His universe. Our soul always seeks evolution and wholeness. When someone experiences an extreme degree of reliance on others, their soul has voluntarily made this choice. This choice of the soul had a purpose. When we experience dependence on others it forces us to learn how to be humble and accept the kindness and love of others. It causes us to experience receiving instead of giving. It moves us to the depths of authentic love, which truly is God's Love.

Do the exercises at the end of this chapter to fully engage, using conscious actions to put this information into your life.

Exercises for Chapter 8

1. You love your loved one that is dying very much. What can you be doing now, while they are still alive to enrich your relationship? Write your answers down and make a plan to commit to follow through.

2. Sometimes you feel like you should not leave your house, or at least not for any length of time away from your loved one. You know that they can be left for a while. Explore why you feel this way. Should you do anything different?

9
Love

There is power in Love.
Love can help and heal when nothing else can.
There is power in Love to lift up and liberate when nothing else will.
Rev. Michael Curry

Love is not only an Element of Spirituality; it is the most important Element of Spirituality. Love is the sum total of all there really is. Love comes first. Love comes last. The Bible tells us so and explains it this way, *"Love is patient; love is kind; love is not envious or boastful or arrogant or rude. It does not insist on its own way; it is not irritable or resentful; it does not rejoice in wrong-doing but rejoices in the truth. It bears all things, believes all things, hopes all things, endures all things."* 1 Corinthians 13:4-7

Eben Alexander (2014) explains that, *"The Universe is based on Love, but if we have no love in ourselves, the Universe will be shut off from us. This is due to our choice to not love ourselves. If we don't love ourselves, we will spend our lives triumphantly declaring that the spiritual world doesn't exist because we have failed to awaken the love within ourselves that alone will render the most obvious of facts visible to us. You cannot come bringing only a superficial sliver of yourself, while your larger, deeper self is left behind. If you want to see all of Heaven, you have to bring all of yourself. This takes honesty and truthfulness. You cannot come to truth dishonestly."*

Alexander explains that your choice to not love yourself was exactly that, your choice… not God's choice. Remember, God is love. As we become more spiritual, we become closer to God. As we remain aware and watch our progress in becoming more spiritual, allowing the "Heaven" in ourselves to unfold, the more we become whole. This is because it brings us to the awareness that we are all one.

The period of anticipatory grieving is a perfect time to learn, understand, and become aware of our actions and thoughts which is why it is not only a blessing, but a gift as well in so many ways. It gives us time to not only explore but to practice over and over. Do not think of the times you have experienced coming up against a problem or situation over and over as a "test" by God for God to see if we learned it or not. Punishing us is not something God does. Not only does God not punish you, but He doesn't judge you either. Instead look at these times as opportunities to practice. God is giving us practice time. God only loves us as he provides the opportunities for us to reach our spiritual goals — to learn the spiritual lessons that we wanted to learn during our lifetime.

Growing spiritually happens in a series of small steps. As with everything else in Earth's lessons, it is best that we practice. Going through anticipatory grieving gives us our abundance of time to practice — to experience, learn, and perfect our ability to show compassion, love, and keep harmony in our lives as well as the life of our loved one. Doing something once, like showing compassion, is not enough to then say, "I have learned that now. I can forget having to do that again." Doing it over and over is the way to change yourself into a more spiritual person. God knows this and he wants us to know and accept it too.

This process is not always easy. But we know that in time it will become easier. We will become who we are at the soul level. We realize that we have grown, when we see that we are calmer, more loving, and happier. When our automatic response to the stressors that used to bring an angry reaction, will now bring one of quiet, loving, calmness, and a simple release of the stress. Practice, "Let it go!" and accept that, "It is, so let it be!"

The "new you" is no longer quick to anger and the new, more spiritual you is someone you like better as you show compassion, love, and create harmony in your midst. Others will also start to see you in a different light, and love and compassion will grow as they see your example. Don't be surprised if your loved one becomes nicer too. As you change and improve, they mirror you and also improve.

We are honored by another poem by Richard Campbell:

Love

Love is teaching.
Love will get the word around.
Love will be what makes people want to listen.
Love is what people want to share.
Love is easy as long as you love yourself first.
Just love not hate.

Richard N. Campbell

Will the episodes that cause stress ever be gone entirely during this wait? No, not likely, but you will have created a new you and respond to the stressors with the new you. Focus on responding not reacting. Each time you are able to do this, you are growing more spiritual. You are living from the inside out; living from your soul's vibrational level. Just consider our human, societal way of thinking or doing something, then compare it with the spiritual way of thinking and doing something. Be wise, choose the spiritual way, which is found inside of you at your soul's vibrational level. This is living from the inside as I have mentioned several times before in this book.

Many believe that we will all go to Heaven. But will that be the same place for all of us? The Bible tells us that Jesus said there are many mansions in Heaven. The Bible also talks of Hell, which is a concept that is hard for many to imagine really exists. Many prefer to believe that everyone, yes, even murderers, all of the low life of earth will go to Heaven. To do anything else is just not describing a loving response from God. God is Love!

We can see that it is conceivable that the more love you have in your heart is likely the ticket to the highest mansions in Heaven. So, where you go, which mansion, is determined by the amount of love in your heart, for love is the essence of Heaven. Love is that of which Heaven is made. Therefore, the murderers may go to a lower vibratory mansion, but they will go to Heaven.

Love is the doorway to enlightenment, the means to growing spiritually. When you start loving yourself you are opening the door to growth. Love your humanity as well as your divinity. Love all of you, even your imperfections. After all, it is the imperfections that are leading you to notice that you can do better in creating a happier life. You won't change the imperfections by denying or hating them. The way to change them is to love them. As you love your negative feelings, they can evolve into positive feelings and it turns them into positive expressions.

Work at putting a positive thought alongside a negative one and know that one positive thought can cancel out hundreds of negative thoughts. Say to yourself, "I'm glad I had that negative feeling or action, because now I see that I could have done better, and I will do better next time." Apologize to others if you have done something that has hurt another. Admit guilt and vow to do better.

As you are thinking about loving others, think first about how much you love yourself. Maureen Moss (2002) reminds us that, *"We will never experience the love of another to a degree greater than the love we are able to give to ourselves. The measure of our past love or current love is in direct proportion to the love we give (or do not give) to ourselves. You don't need to change yourself. You only need to love yourself. Start by loving where you are right now in your spiritual growth. As you love yourself, you grow spiritually by moving into higher and higher levels of consciousness."*

"The rewards of spiritual growth are many," according to Sanaya Roman (1989) *"a clearer sense of direction, a greater feeling of being in control, and a deeper understanding of why things are happening. There is an increasing calm that comes as you begin to enjoy and understand your life. You can truly live a life that is joyful and loving to yourself. Practice extending this love to your relationships. Ask yourself what is the higher purpose of this phone call or this visit? How can I make a contribution to this person's life? How can my work, product, advice, or service empower this person?"*

Melanie Barnum (2016) helps us to understand that, *"God's Universe is full of entities that will help us love and grow spiritually."* She lists them below.

- *Deceased Relatives share many personal messages with us*

- *Spirit Guides help direct us in life*
- *Angels tend to be around for life lessons and emergencies*
- *Ascended Masters work in the background, helping us gently towards enlightenment*
- *All are operating out of pure unconditional love.*

    As you approach your encounters with others think of it as "service to others." Make it an everyday occurrence. Think of it as becoming who you are. You will lift your relationships to a higher level and you yourself will evolve more rapidly. The other person will feel your love and encouragement. Make sure it is sincere on your part. Really live it and you will find many wonderful surprises and business successes as you focus your attention on serving others.

    The term, "Namaste" is a term used often in spiritual circles. It means, "I honor the place in you where we are all one." It is used as a greeting or salutation in written messages. Since it is not a mainstream word, you could still silently begin telling others "Namaste" in order to remind yourself to love everyone as your own children. Practice benevolence, mercy and compassion, always forgiving them as soon as something happens that seems to be wrong. Let it go, toss it into the imaginary river flowing in front of you, never to see it again because it is going down stream and you are going up stream. By doing this you will keep love in your heart for others and continue to give loving service to others.

    Og Mandino is quoted as saying, *"Beginning today, treat everyone you meet as if they were going to be dead by midnight. Extend to them all the care, kindness, and understanding you can muster, and do so with no thought of any reward. Your life will never be the same."*

He continues to say, *"If you were on your death bed would there be one single thing more important to you in your final moments than being loved or having loved well? I think not."*

Is that not what we are dealing with here with this time frame of anticipatory grief? While we are in this period of anticipatory grief we can focus on love. In fact, there is no greater thing that we can focus on. Love now because it will bring us lasting peace when our loved one dies, which for many reading this book, that could be by midnight tonight. Take Og Mandino's words to heart and truly love your loved one. Even in anticipatory grief, the time is short, no matter how long it takes for them to die, we know it is coming.

Love will bring you to greater spiritual levels as you grow in spirituality. The long anticipatory grief period is really a gift. It gives us time to love and grow spiritually. We are blessed to have so much time with our loved one. Many things can be talked about, smoothing the way ahead for them and for you. Love paves the road for them to gain courage to let go of their worldly life and physical body here on earth and to prepare themselves for a new residence in Heaven. Love will pave the way for you to grow spiritually and for you to have a smoother time adjusting to life without them after they are gone. Growing spiritually will bring you peace.

Love is the most important thing on your journey. Love is all that is needed. If you have God's love in your heart, you have it all. Remember, as Marianne Williamson (2004) has said, *"Love is the only way we can transcend darkness and love is the only way we ever will."*

Return to your journal and do the exercises for this chapter.

Exercises for Chapter 9

1. Think about the term Spiritual Love. Take some time to write about what it really means to you.

2. What three things can you do to help yourself grow more spiritual thus more loving? (i.e., plan a meditating routine, read spiritual books, be one with nature, more quiet time for self, practice, practice, practice). Think of at least one that is not listed as examples.

PART 3

Elements of Love

Introduction to Part 3
Elements of Love

Part Three contains information about identifying and explaining the Elements of Love. When we better understand what the Elements of Love are, we will be better able to practice love consciously.

In this section, we will break love down piece by piece and then work on each piece separately. Focusing on each, we become the true masters of love that God and our soul wants us to be.

We will discuss at least ten different aspects of love. That is not to say that there are only ten. If you come up with additional ones, then bless you. Elements of love overlap so much that at times it is hard to talk about just one and not mention one or more of the others.

Since there isn't a specific order to list the individual Elements of Love, for this book, we will start with grace.

10
Grace

God is able to make all grace abound to you,
So that having all sufficiency in all things at all times,
You may abound in every good work.
2 Corinthians 2:8

Grace is an Element of Love. It is God's all empowering force that leads us to peace; the peace of mind, body and soul. While we are in the throes of the anticipatory grieving period on our own journey, grace can surround us and give us the energy and the will to carry on, no matter how long it takes to reach the end of this particular part of our journey. Grace is a sweet, loving and protective shield around us. It is God's love giving us the strength to do what must be done on the earthly plane and also gives us guidance to grow spiritually during this hard time in our life.

Deepak Chopra (2009) explains it this way, *"Grace is the all-embracing power of God. (Abundance, purity, unconditioned love, a gift freely given.) Grace abolishes life's limitations. There is nothing to be guilty of. The whole issue of good vs evil disappears. Peace is no longer a dream to be chased, but an innate quality of the heart. Grace, like the soul itself, steps down God's infinite power to human scale. It carries more than a whiff of magic as befits a total transformation."*

Grace is a soothing balm on our emotions. When we ask for the White Light to surround us before meditation, it is God's grace that brings us the White Light. When we pray, it is grace that brings us quietness and to a place of reverence. It is Grace that carries our prayer to the universe and to God. It is grace that brings us the answers to our prayers. Grace is an Element of Love that brings us to a state of serenity. It opens the door and allows more love to come into our heart, and more light to come into your soul, to help us move closer to God.

Grace is the unmerited mercy that God gave to humanity. It is the unconditional love of God for us, exactly as we are, apart from our own efforts. Grace reassures us that we have no worries about our present state of being. God loves us and gives us His grace.

Grace will be there for us when we are ready to receive it. God won't force it upon us. Nor will God hold it back from us. God will always send grace, but we must be ready and willing to receive it. When we want grace to enter our presence and our inner soul, we can just quiet our mind by closing our eyes and ask God for it. Then wait to feel the calmness, the assurance, and the love of God. God will send grace when you have your spiritual energy at the right level to receive from Heaven's greatness. When you realize that you are surrounded by grace, you can know that a holy instant just happened, and you have connected with God.

Yes, the grace of God will surround you and carry you through. Call on grace when you feel you are getting angry, call on grace when you are feeling sad. It is okay to cry. Grace will wash away your tears and bring you peace and a better understanding of the situation. You can do it! You can carry on through the grace of God.

Use your journal to better explore this concept of grace in your life.

Exercises for Chapter 10

1. What does the Element of Love called grace mean to you?

2. Have you experienced the feeling of grace in your lifetime?

3. List at least two times that you know you were feeling the grace of God. How did you feel?

4. If you have not experienced or recognized the grace of God yet, what can you do to bring the experience of this wonderful gift from God. (For example, before you meditate, ask God to surround you with the White Light of the Holy Spirit. Wait for it, then feel it, see it, experience the White Light. God's grace brought it to you.)

11
Compassion

*I have just three things to teach:
simplicity, patience, compassion.
These three are your greatest treasures.*
Lao Tzu

If anticipatory grief can be envisioned as a spiritual teacher, then its most profound lesson is compassion. Anticipatory grieving allows us an excellent time to develop spiritually through the powerful Element of Love called compassion. No one is exempt from spiritual development. We soon realize that life is fleeting, very short, in the overall scheme of things. We realize that all that we hold dear will soon decay. It doesn't matter if we are rich or poor, young or old, healthy or ill, none of us is exempt from an inner need to develop spiritually. To do this we must try to live compassionate, meaningful lives.

To have a life steeped in compassion, we must begin where we are in this very moment, in all our relationships. It happens *now*. In other words, live in the moment of now and accept what *is*. *Let it Be!* Accept whatever is happening and look for the good in it. Be open to thinking about your anger, hurt, or disagreement with the situation and move forward to a calmer understanding in your mind and heart.

Have compassion for *YOU*. You do matter… what you wanted in life does matter. You may have to make an adjustment to your wants list, but for now, relax and look around you for what is good right now. There is good in everything that comes into your life, we just have to take time and look for it. If you look, you will find the good and then be grateful and have compassion for yourself and all of those around you.

In order to understand compassion, one must experience it directly. Reading about it, being told about it, and/or seeing it acted out by another will not get you to where you need to be for yourself to fully understand and feel compassion. The rewards from both giving compassion and receiving it, are many. It has been said that compassion is the doorway to grace. We just talked about grace...look back to Chapter 10 if you need to review grace again with this in mind.

Compassion involves showing sympathy and concern for others. It activates emotions and behaviors that can be described in many ways. Compassion may involve emotions such as: being sensitive, tender hearted, loving, gentle, soft hearted, thoughtful, merciful, warm hearted, lenient, tolerant, considerate, kind, humane, charitable, benevolent, good natured and many more. As we look at our life and how we interact with others, we can make an assessment as to whether we are compassionate or not.

Compassion is one of the highest of all of the energy attractor power patterns. Our capacity to understand, forgive, and accept is directly linked to our ability to have compassion. It brings us peace of mind and heart. Compassion is more than feeling sorry for someone (having pity) or commiserating with them. You actually feel the pain and struggles of others as though they were your own. You work to end the suffering of another.

The word compassion is made up of two parts: com, meaning "with," and passion, which means "emotions, energy or in some way intense activity." Therefore, compassion implies an active sharing of an experience, thus alleviation of suffering in part because you shared your heart felt sensitive, spiritual love with them. It brings comfort to the other party. This can be human, pet, plants and more, including the compassion that you give to yourself.

Looking for ways to grow your compassion will enhance your spiritual growth. There are so many opportunities during the period of anticipatory grieving for us to practice increasing your compassion. Waiting for your loved one to die is not easy. Yet, this is an excellent time to help you grow spiritually, as long as you look to your spiritual path for relief from your pain of grief.

Sameet M. Kumar (2005) reminds us of this truism, *"Appreciate that most of your spiritual growth occurs **not** when you are at ease, comfortable, in your life and relationships, but when you are suffering."* Spiritual growth and practice are like a soothing balm on an open sore. Compassion is easy when we are surrounded by loved ones and life is going well. The true test and challenge to living a spiritual life is having compassion towards others and ourselves during difficult times, such as when you feel depressed, anxious, irritated, hurt or angry.

With compassion, we can see that the difficult person that is causing us problems is really our spiritual teacher. Imagine that you are seeing through their human actions and see them as their spiritual soul. Their soul is beautiful and loving. Take solace and know that they need more of your soul's love to calm their hurt and anger that is being directed at you. This takes practice. It takes a true belief and growth in your ability to have compassion for others. Forgive them on the spot, don't let these things build up and become bricks of emotion to deal with later. Forgive now. Show compassion now. Practice compassion and plant seeds of compassion in every relationship, good or bad.

Use your journal to write your thoughts to the exercises for this chapter.

Exercises for Chapter 11

1. What does compassion look like to you?

2. List at least three times that you have felt compassion for yourself in this past month.

3. List at least three times that you have felt compassion for others this past month.

4. What three things you can do to grow compassion?

5. How will you practice compassion, right now?

   Remember: Practice, Practice, Practice.

12
Harmony

*Always aim at complete harmony of thought
and words and deed.
Always aim at purifying your thoughts
and everything will be well.*
                    — Mahatma Gandhi

Harmony is another Element of Love and is the result of our positive thinking and actions. The Sages of Spirituality all have messages to share regarding how to have harmony with ourselves when we are alone, or with relationships when we are with others. The secret seems to be very simple as stated by the great Indian philosopher and spiritual teacher, J. Krishnamurt. This is his powerful message: *"This is my secret;* ***I don't mind what happens.****"* This is equal to my own conclusion for growth in dealing with things that seem to upset me at first glance. I say to myself, "It doesn't matter." I find it amazing how fast my emotions change, and I can truly have and show compassion which brings harmony to the situation for me and others.

This didn't happen overnight for me. It took thoughtful and willful practice along with a strong desire for harmony in all that I do. Am I always successful? No, of course not. I am human too, one that is just trying to improve myself, just like most other humans. But we must do more than just think of improving ourselves for the sake of improvement. We must always strive to improve in a more conscious spiritual way to have a happier life of harmony.

Eckhart Tolle (2005) shares his thoughts regarding the statement by J. Krishnamurt above. *"This statement implies that I am in alignment with what happens. "What Happens," of course, refers to the suchness of this moment, which always is as it is. It refers to content, the form that this moment, the only moment there ever **is**, takes. What does this mean? It means that to have harmony we must be in alignment, in agreement, to allow whatever is happening to happen, allow it to "Be." We do not judge right or wrong, good or bad, it just is."*

Tolle is talking about the moment "*Now.*" In society we are trained from childhood to judge everything in our world. Does the fear of loss of control of your world cause your ego to take charge when you think of doing this practice of allowing everything that happens to just *be*? Start practicing harmony now. It will form a basis for your actions with the outcome to be harmonious in all you do and especially with your relationships. Practice alignment with what "*is.*" Put yourself into a state of inner non-resistance with what happens. No labels, no judgement, just be in the "*now*" moment of what "*is.*"

Does this mean you can no longer take action to bring about change in your life? Tolle states that, *"On the contrary when the basis for your actions is inner alignment with the present moment, your actions become empowered by the intelligence of life itself."* If you are in alignment with God internally, you will enjoy seeing the outcome as one of harmony instead of anger or hurt. There is always more than one way, more than your way to get to a solution. When harmony is the goal many solutions come to mind and in time the best solution comes to the surface. Harmony leaves us feeling good about ourselves and others. It does, however, involve letting go of the ego and pushing it to the background of your consciousness.

Great relationships are not created by only one big event. It takes many, many small seemingly insignificant happenings to make a great relationship. It is a series of choices we make on a daily basis to love, to forgive, to be trustworthy, to be kind and considerate to others and ourselves. You can create harmony where the opposite is in play. Your words and actions can be used to heal the situation and help others to feel empowered. Harmony brings joy to your heart and a smile to your face. You can experience seeing others look at you with love in their eyes and happiness in their soul.

When we find ourselves in the long-term grieving situation, we have many opportunities to work on harmony. Because one of the most prominent situations we experience when caring for a love one, is the seemingly constant stream of interruptions. These interruptions often cause us to become angry, which is only a natural human reaction. But we can view all the interruptions as opportunities to grow spiritually and put into practice changing how we act towards our loved one. We can respond in a learned way (instead of reacting) by using understanding, patience, and love to get us through it. We can just let it be and see it as an opportunity to experience compassion. Life is better after experiencing compassion that brings harmony. Your loved one feels good as opposed to how they (and you) would have felt if you had quickly reacted with anger. You have created harmony where there might have been dis-harmony. It is in your control.

Yes, harmony is an Element of Love that leads you to "feel" yourself being kind, tolerant, and non-stressed. When you feel harmony, it is a good feeling. We already know that all harmony and/or stress is internally generated by one's attitudes. David Hawkins (2002) tells us that, *"It isn't life's events, but one's reaction to them, that activates the symptoms of stress."* We could add to that quote, symptoms of stress *or "harmony."* When we are stressed, we have allowed dis-harmony to enter our space. Although we are not always in control of what enters our space, we are in control how we deal with our space. We always determine what behavior we will display, and we can learn to allow harmony to take the lead even when we feel stressed.

Reacting to stress keeps us from having harmony in our lives. Learn to respond to stress instead of reacting. Reacting is often a habit whereas responding is a learned behavior as you think through how to let it be! You must, however, practice that new learned behavior over and over.

Be proud of yourself because you created higher energy vibrations of harmony instead of the lower vibrations of anger and hurt. You and your soul just grew more spiritual in the process. Your relationships just improved.

Let it be in the now. Only if you resist the now are you at the mercy of what happens. The world will determine your happiness/unhappiness, your harmony/dis-harmony. No resistance, just observance is the best policy. Allow the universe to do its job. Learning patience to do this is essential. Not personalizing events will help you see that you are not a victim.

Harmony is another word for peacefulness. You will feel free and peaceful if you strive for harmony in all situations. Be completely at one with the event, with no resistance, and the event will have no power over you. In seconds you will feel harmony.

Go to your journal and write your thoughts on harmony.

Exercises for Chapter 12

1. What does harmony mean to you?

2. When was the last time that you were completely aware of a situation where you started out being angry and turned it into harmony?

3. Write about how your emotions changed when you decided to have harmony instead of anger.

4. Write about how the tension in your space and that of others in the room with you changed to one of peace when you pushed your ego back and took a spiritual stance in the situation.

13
Wisdom

All human wisdom is summed up in two words;
wait and hope.
Alexandre Dumas

What is wisdom and where do we find it? Wisdom, as an Element of Love, is what happens when our understanding of a thing deepens to the point that it changes our behavior. Wisdom comes in many forms and opportunities. Sonia Croquette (2008) shares her thoughts on this subject. *"Wisdom is the knowledge that only those choices in life that bring us closer to God and Divine Mind are of any value. Those [choices] that take away from Divine Mind are harmful… not only to us, but to everyone."*

Eckhart Tolle (2003) shares some of his wisdom with us when he says, *"Wisdom comes with the ability to be still. Just look and just listen. No more is needed. Being still, looking, and listening activates the non-conceptual intelligence within you. Let stillness direct your words and actions."*

Every day we are given chances to become wiser. They come when we are cut off in traffic or someone says something that ticks us off. Becoming wiser is all about examining our behavior and making a choice as to how best to respond to the same situation in the future so that we can remain in the Divine Mind more. We may not be successful each and every time, but we will be growing wiser as we try. Wisdom comes from within (inside ourselves). Knowledge comes from outside of ourselves.

Learning our earthly lessons is another way we gain wisdom. Teresa Caputo (2015) says, *"Learning lessons isn't about being perfect; it's about recognizing that your time here unfolds the way it's meant to, as you make choices that fulfill you. You gain something much harder to earn and more valuable... Wisdom."*

Perfection is a myth that humans continually try to accomplish and yet fail because perfection doesn't exist. Transform your thinking so that you can come from a Divine point of view, rather than the human mind's point of view. Wisdom is when we find ourselves in a "bad place" emotionally and it is then more important that we be devoted to reminding ourselves of the good we have done and the goodness that we are. Wisdom is reminding ourselves that the greatest contentment we ever felt in our lives is when we wanted nothing. Sit with that just for a moment right now. Experience this moment often. Wisdom comes with time and spiritual growth.

Others may not share your views on morals, values, and convictions, but if your morals, values and convictions speak truth to you, stick to them. It is not loving to force your views on to others. Respect the differences of opinions and perspectives. Use your inner morals and perspectives to live your life by but have the wisdom and sensitivity of other people's rights, too. Always remember the Golden Rule, "Do unto others as you would have them do unto you."

Wisdom is knowing that there is a stream of well-being that is always flowing to us. You can allow it or resist it, but it flows just the same. To allow it means you have the wisdom to be in the right vibrational alignment with it. You cannot stand in resistance of that stream of well-being and at the same time receive it. You must open the flood gates and allow your well-being to flow to you.

Much wisdom can be learned as we are living in the anticipatory time frame. Over and over we are given the opportunity to practice the Elements of Love. As we succeed, we always gain more wisdom about what works and what doesn't. We can perfect our approach to different scenarios and bring more love into the relationship with our loved one that is dying. This wisdom spills over into our other relationships and we have a happier life as a result.

Spend some time thinking about how your wisdom has grown over your lifetime. Use your journal for this book to write your thoughts and solidify this wonderful Element of Love into your future.

Exercises for Chapter 13

1. Think of a time when you realized that you could have done something better because you had already experienced the same thing before and what you did didn't work well. Now you are doing it the same way again even though you knew it didn't work last time.

2. To gain wisdom, we must change how we do things. This is how we learn our lessons of wisdom. Write about how you could do things differently next time you find yourself in the same situation you wrote about above.

14
Forgiveness

*Forgiveness is the fragrance
that the violet sheds
on the heel that has crushed it.*
Mark Twain

There is a saying, "The holiest of all spots on earth is where an ancient hatred has become a present love." The author is unknown to me. The Element of Love called forgiveness is the only action that can bring about this transformation. Forgiveness is not something you do; it is a state of being. When you are in this state of being it brings forth who you really are. You are living from within, living from your soul level.

Baptist De Pape (2014) discusses what forgiveness is not. *"Forgiveness does not mean understanding, defending or approving of another person's behavior or trying to artificially suppress the feeling caused by that behavior. Nor does forgiving mean wiping the other person's behavior from your memory, pretending that the hurt, the humiliation, or the injury never happened. Forgiving means simply opening the door to your heart again and being prepared to abandon the hope, once and for all, that the past could have been different and abandon the hopes of a past without injustice. Forgiveness is not about looking back but about looking ahead. It is about realizing that there is a reason why a car's windshield is a lot bigger than the rearview mirror."*

Forgiveness is one of God's Universal Laws. A person can never grow spiritually if they are holding a grudge. Their heart is not open to receive blessings and teachings from the Heavens (from God). Sanaya Roman (1989) in her wisdom explains that, *"If you are around people or energies that you aren't comfortable with, see them as offering you opportunities for spiritual growth. The thoughts and feelings of people you have the most trouble harmonizing with are the very ones who will give you the most growth. That is why you have attracted them into your life. You can look for and learn to enjoy what is positive about them and find ways to go even higher* [in spiritual energy levels] *when you are around energies that are not as harmonious as your own."*

I discuss forgiveness in my book, "Spiritual Reflections, I Tried, God Helped" (2016). Included within there is a list of quotes that brought me to an understanding of what forgiveness is all about and helped me along with prayer and meditation to grow in the ability to forgive when I felt a great injustice had been forced upon me earlier in my life from a loved one. Looking back, I can now see clearly now that the episode was part of my and my adversary's divine plans. Our destinies were working themselves out providing an opportunity for both of us to grow spiritually.

I'm happy to be able to say that we have a greater understanding now because of the ability to forgive one another, not just tolerate one another. Forgiveness and tolerance for the things you desire to not be around you are closely linked. They seem to go hand-in-hand. Except… you can tolerate without forgiving, but if you forgive you have mastered tolerance. This is an important point to ponder.

In the process of forgiving, my adversary and I both learned to love each other unconditionally. We learned to love without strings attached, without taking everything each said personally. We learned to let it be. No, the past cannot change, but the future is bright and good for our relationship. All we have to do is remember what the experience has taught us. For myself, I say, "It doesn't matter." I refuse to be a victim again. I always have that imaginary river following in front of me. I often just drop the concern along with a prayer into the imaginary river, never to see it again as it floats away from me on down the river. My heart is full of love instead of hate or self-pity. If it does come back, then I know I didn't toss all of it into the river. I just do it again, but this time I really mean it and give all to the river of God's love.

There is an excellent book written by Colin Tipping (2002) called *"Radical Forgiveness,"* that details a wonderful way to learn how to forgive. *"Fake it until you make it!"*, he tells us. *"This really means surrender to the process, putting forth no effort nor trying to control the results."*

In society, it is popular to be a victim. We are taught this from childhood just by watching the adults around us. There was a Seattle study which found that the more effort the participants put into trying to forgive, the more difficult they found it to let go of their hurt and anger. When they stopped trying to control the process, at some point in time, forgiveness just happened because they were open to forgiving.

As long as you think of yourself as a victim, you keep yourself in the victim mode. You have not forgiven. Perhaps you have put it on the back burner and try to not think about it, but when you do think about it, it hurts all over again. Putting something on the back burner is not the same as forgiveness. Make a concerted effort through prayer, meditation and reading books about forgiveness so you can move forward and love them and yourself again. Before you can fully forgive, you must first recognize that you are seeing yourself as a victim and then "Let Go... Let God." When you drop the victim consciousness you can then move forward. You will feel free; you will raise your spiritual energy level back to where you can receive God's blessings again.

The most profound thing for someone to learn is that you can forgive someone for a past deed and yet, not be obligated to get involved with them in the future. It is not necessary to give them more chances to hurt you again and again. Focus on love and kindness towards them. Know that you have forgiven them. Know that you don't have a need to continue to bash them to others because you feel neutral towards them. That is all that is necessary for you to move on in your quest for traveling your own spiritual journey. You will have grown in spirituality and your soul will have grown too.

Tipping reminds us that, *"The energetic imprint of Radical Forgiveness is the willingness to be open to the idea that there is nothing to forgive."* Just as with everything else in life, everything is as it is supposed to be. All the difficult things come into our life to help us learn the lessons that we came to learn. When the need to forgive comes into our life, you can be sure that there is a lesson that God's Universe is leading us to. We learn best when life is difficult, not when everything is going smooth.

When you see these things coming, as we so often do during the anticipatory grief, embrace them and move through them with grace. You will have all the help you need from God and His Universe, if you ask for it. Don't fight it, lean into it using all the love that surrounds you, even asking for more love to help you through it. You will come out on the other side feeling good, not bad and your soul will have grown too.

Sometimes our loved one says things that hurts us while they are trying to adjust to what is happening to them in their life's journey on this road to dying. Forgive them now. Take each day one at a time. Forgive as you go, don't store it up inside you. Forgive as it happens. Forgiveness of the present is actually more important than forgiveness of the past. If you allow forgiveness now, allowing it to be as it is, then there will be no accumulation of resentment that needs to be forgiven later. Stay in the now. Make sure your "now" is "love" and it is coming from your heart center. If you feel the emotion of love, you can't feel the emotion of hate at the same time. Where there is love, there can be no hate. This will make each day of your journey through anticipatory grieving go smoother and with no regrets later after your loved one is gone.

Again, go to your journal and spend some time on the exercises.

Exercises for Chapter 14

1. Do you find it hard to forgive someone, or do you forgive easily?

2. Think of the last time that you forgave someone. How long did it take, seconds or weeks?

3. What were your feelings after you decided to forgive? (It does take a decision on your part to forgive.)

4. Do you have an ongoing feud with someone currently? Think of how you feel. Do you like being a victim? Do you find pleasure in nursing your wounds? Do you want the other person to hurt like you do?

5. Is this situation taking a long time to get over? Are you gaining something by not forgiving this person? If so, what? How are you benefiting from this non-forgiving?

6. What are your fears, concerns, etc.? Is it easier to forgive if you know it is okay for you to forgive a past action and that you are not obligated to get involved with them in the future to prove that you forgave? To forgive doesn't mean that we have to give them another chance to hurt us. We can be around them but not get involved emotionally, yet be kind, even be compassionate towards them.

7. How will you know when you have really forgiven someone? For example, can you be in the same room with them and interact with love and kindness, but not commit to future plans, etc.?

15
Patience

*Patience is the calm acceptance
that things can happen
in a different order
than the one you have in mind.*

David G. Allen

Patience is an Element of Love because it keeps us from moving too fast, expecting everything we want will be given to us immediately. There is value in waiting, making sure all pieces are in place and we are doing the right thing for all concerned. Patience is not selfish, although procrastination can be. There is a difference between patience and procrastination. Procrastination is a deliberate act of not doing something now when it should be done now, and then pushing it into the future to be done at a later date. This can become a habit and so often, the something doesn't ever get done and leads to laziness. So often that is the person's intention in the first place. Whereas patience is pushing something into the future to wait until the right time arrives. The intention is to actually do the something, but when it is best for all concerned. Patience is waiting for God's Divine timing.

Iyanla Vanzant (2001) says, *"Patience is a choice. It is the conscious choice to be reliant on the unceasing movement of life. Patience is an ability. It is the mental ability to remember that once the wheels start turning and the movement has begun, the destination will surely be reached… eventually."*

Patience is a skill that is learned. It must be practiced over and over to be really good at it. It is the emotional skill of learning to know that what you desire, will happen exactly when it needs to happen. It is learning to be flexible and allowing some changes from what we first desired to happen. We must learn to be at peace with how the universe presents this desired thing to happen. This is so, even though it has happened in a different way than we thought it would. It is trusting that what, when, where, and how it does happen will be in our best interest and also in the best interest for all others involved.

Patience can be thought of as a science. It is the spiritual science of using your mental and emotional skills of creation to such an exacting degree that the outcome is asserted at the beginning. It is the science of knowing what you set in motion with your mind, what you believe in your heart, what you praise in your soul will happen at just the right time, in just the right way.

When we are patient, it speaks volumes of love to those around us and to our soul. "Hurry, hurry" changes everything to a high emotional state and a lower spiritual one. It is best to believe that waiting has a reason, therefore having patience brings us contentment, while we wait. We are not in control of anything except ourselves and how we behave. During anticipatory grief there is much waiting and having patience will help us get through it in a more loving way.

We grow spiritually when we learn to wait patiently as the poem "Wait" at the beginning of the book states. Patience helps us to learn to know God. When we are patient our soul is growing too.

Write in your journal to consider how you would describe patience and accept it as an Element of Love.

Exercises for Chapter 15

1. Describe what patience means to you.

2. Are you a patient person or impatient?

3. Describe a recent time when you were impatient with someone and because of it, harmony was lost for that event.

4. Think of a recent time when you realized that you were feeling impatient emotionally but knew that dealing with the problem in this manner would not be good for you or the other person and you drew on your strongest point to be patient instead. How did it turn out? Were you able to keep harmony in your interaction with another? If so, you grew spiritually.

16
Spiritual Courage

*Courage is knowing
what not to fear.*
Plato

One might not think of courage as an Element of Love, but it is the force that propels us forward in our quest to become more spiritual, more loving. Courage helps us get through the period of anticipatory grief. It is the driving force to keep us from getting deeply depressed. Courage keeps us going through these trying times. Courage, in itself, means being brave by overriding the fears of our own ego.

Spiritual courage is a journey that requires you to be in the present. You become a witness to your own attachments and learn how to self-correct. You learn to surrender your ego to a higher level of courage consciousness by setting a declaration of courageous intentions. Personal courage means not letting your own fears overcome your goals and define who you are. No one wants to be defined by their fears. Setting intentions before undertaking changes in our life helps us stay on track and have a successful outcome.

Sonia Choquette (2008) shares her thoughts on courage. *"'Lionhearted' vibrationally is a vibration of clarity, purpose, and commitment that nothing would dare interrupt. To have courage of this magnitude only comes with unwavering focus, and commitment to what Spirit requires, unwavering focus on our goal. The courageous heart sits its course and doesn't ask in fear and doubt how it will achieve its goals. The how's reveal themselves as the process unfolds. Courage is the heart of action, not hesitation."*

Physical courage is bravery in the face of physical pain, hardship, death or threat of death. Courage requires an ability to be dangerously unselfish. Spiritual courage is the ability to act rightly in the face of popular opposition, shame, scandal, discouragement, or personal loss. During our anticipatory grief, we need to call upon both physical courage and spiritual courage to help us get through these trying times.

Courage is the quality of mind or spirit that enables a person to bravely face difficulty, danger, pain, and deep sadness in spite of fear. Have the courage of your convictions to act in accordance with your beliefs, especially in spite of criticism. Criticism can cause us to react poorly. Have the courage to live what you believe.

The virtue of fortitude is also translated to mean courage, however, it includes the aspects of perseverance and patience. Certainly, we need all three during the trying time of anticipatory grieving.

Your decision to grow spiritually sometimes causes you to make some changes in your behavior. Others around you, often family members, may take notice. They may not be ready to join you or to even to have you change. They may set up some resistance or ridicule you in your new thoughts and behaviors. This is when courage comes into play. Be patient with those that do not agree with your choices. Love them, but then have courage to continue on. In time they will see that this is best for you and that you are not trying to get them to join you in new beliefs or actions. If they don't accept this about you, you may have to make some hard choices to limit your time around them.

Set your spiritual intention to have a quiet resolve to carry on in your endeavor to become more spiritual. Pray for courage to walk on, day by day in this season of your life. Others may not understand what it is like to live in a state of sadness and emotional pain for an extended period of time. Others may not know what this feels like and make judgements regarding your behavior. But keep on, keeping on. Allow God to direct you as this is part of your destiny. Accept it as such and move on by putting one foot in front of the other until this situation plays itself out to the end.

All that happens is meant to happen. Allow yourself to grow spiritually. Spirituality provides a purpose--a reason to not give up. You are learning to be kinder, more understanding, more calm, happier even in this situation of sadness. God will give you courage to do His will if you ask for help from Him and His universe.

Be an example of a person that uses their courage to encourage others in their challenges in life. Write poetry, music, lyrics to that music or write a book to help others and yourself. Use your courage to sooth the savage beast of the illness of which your loved one is suffering and realize how it has changed your life as well as theirs. It will all pay off after they are gone. Wait, just as God says, use your courage to wait just as the poem in chapter one says.

God and His universe will help you to be more courageous than you think you can be.

Do the exercises for this chapter to work out in your mind the details of your feelings and find a way to be courageous while on this extraordinary journey. Being courageous will help you in all facets of your life now and in the future.

Exercises for Chapter 16

1. Where do you stand on the scale of bravery? Are you able to be courageous or do you sink into cowardness when faced with hardship?

2. Think about the last time that you were ridiculed about your beliefs. What did you do about it?

3. Do you have a plan on how to be courageous in the face of ridicule over your beliefs? Do it now. Set your intentions to be brave and face the personal storm that others bring to you when they do not agree with your choices to be different than they are in your beliefs. Remember that God and His universe will help you. Give it time. Give them time to see how much happier you are and how this change has been better for you as you believe the way you want to believe.

4. Have a talk with God right now and ask Him to help you.

17
Gratitude

Thankfulness is the beginning of gratitude.
Gratitude is the completion of Thankfulness.
Thankfulness may consist merely of words.
Gratitude is shown in acts.
                               Henri Frederic Amiel

    Gratitude is a special Element of Love that helps us along our journey through anticipatory grief. Being grateful is opening the door to having greater happiness. When we open our hearts to find something to be grateful for daily, we find room in our thinking to become more open to more love rather than when we are only having negative thoughts. It places us on a special level of spiritual energy that opens our hearts and minds to receive from God and His universe.

    Linda Howe (2016) shares her thoughts, saying, *"Gratitude is the result of a choice, an act of will. Once we decide to consider the option of being grateful no matter what transpires, we place ourselves in a position to receive all the good that can possibly come from a situation."*

    Anticipatory grieving is included in just this kind of situation. Being grateful for the opportunity of being with your loved one longer and being grateful to see this time as a blessing will put you in the position to receive all the good that can possibly be had from this scenario. Being grateful helps us to make the day brighter and lighter for everyone in our mists, not just ourselves. It raises the spiritual vibrations for others as well. If nothing else, remember that it raises the spiritual vibrations for you and makes your life easier.

Howe continues, *"Even when we are tangled up in disaster, the moment we muster the willingness to be grateful, we align with all the possibilities inherent in these circumstances. To move forward in your life, direct your attention to gratitude and then let it take the reins. There is no need to push yourself ahead or force your circumstances... that won't work over the long haul anyway. Focus on being thankful and sincere, and you will travel into the heart of ever-expanding goodness."*

You may ask the question, "How can this grieving ever be good for me?" Howe continues to explain, *"From a soul level perspective, every person, place and thing... absolutely everything that comes to pass, without exception, is in your life to support you in developing your soul level awareness."*

Gratitude during your grieving brings you to a closer walk with God. What about our loved one or those family members that are not accepting of the situation, blaming the doctor, nurses, you or others? You may ask how can I help them to grow spiritually too and have more peace with this anticipatory grieving situation? Well, you may not be able to help them, except through example. Remember that we are not responsible for how others feel or think about a situation. We can only control ourselves, our own thoughts and our own responses.

Release those thoughts if your attempts have not worked. Whether a situation or circumstance is good for another person is not your concern. Your ability to help or benefit others is always the result of what is good for you because when you are blessed, those around you are blessed also. Their experience of blessing is not within your control, you do not get to determine their experience.

If your family continues to remain negative, perhaps even acting hateful toward you, then recognize and know that in some way, somehow, a painful interaction with another person is good for you. It is giving something to you, teaching you, helping you grow, and allowing you to move through the energy paralysis that comes from perceiving yourself as a victim. Be grateful for this opportunity to grow spiritually, because you are practicing forgiveness and love toward everyone through these trying times.

Negative experiences give us knowledge and contributes to our spiritual development. Our most severe challenges will one day reveal themselves to be our greatest teachers. But why is it taking so long for my loved one to die, you may ask. The answer to that question is that **nothing ever goes away until it has taught us what we need to know.** We learn more from the difficult times in our lives. We are more alert as we search for solace and peace.

Esther and Jerry Hicks (2004) tells us, *"Think only positive thoughts because when you "expect" something, it is on the way. When you "believe" something, it is on the way, just as when you "fear" something it is on the way."* Therefore, think only positive thoughts. Do be careful of what you are saying, as YOU are listening. We become what we think, expect, believe, or even fear.

Use your Emotional Guidance System (EGS) to guide you. This is similar to the well-known GPS systems we are all so familiar with when we travel. When you go inside your heart and emotions to find an answer or make a decision, you are using your EGS to guide you. Spirit will help you when you ask.

There is no condition so severe that you cannot reverse it by choosing different thoughts. However, choosing different thoughts requires a decision to focus and practice. If you continue to focus the same way you have been, then nothing will change in your experience. Stop pushing. Stop being angry. Stop blaming. Just change your thoughts to being grateful for this experience and see this long wait as a blessing — as something that is in your best interest.

Be grateful for each additional day you are able to be with your loved one. Look for things to be grateful for, instead of looking at all of this as a negative. Love them more, love yourself more. It will make everything easier when the time comes that you no longer have them with you. Remember, this too shall pass in Divine time and what you will have left is a greater capacity to love and to be stronger spiritually. Accept it. Let it be. Give it your best effort to be grateful.

Go to your journal and spend some time thinking about how being grateful can change your life.

Exercises for Chapter 17

1. Make a list of things you are grateful for right now in your everyday life.

2. Make a list of what you perceive as being something that you are sure is <u>not</u> good for you that is happening in your life right now.

3. Compare the lists. Look for areas where you can turn at least one negative thing into a positive by being grateful.

4. Make a plan on how you are going to work on being more grateful on a daily basis. Meditate on this today and every day.

18
Unconditional Love

Unconditional love really exists in each of us.
It is part of our inner being.
It is not so much an active emotion as a state of being.
It is not "I love you" for this or that reason,
not "I love you if you love me."
Its love for no reason,
love without object.
Ram Doss

Unconditional Love is not only an Element of Love but an essential part of our spiritual being.
In unconditional love, there is absolutely no anxiety or insecurity possible. You are loved because you are "you." True love is non-possessive. Love is beyond the body. Love flows through you constantly as you begin to mature. This love expresses itself in every word, action, and thought throughout our lives.

When we let go of our ego is when we can find true love. Love is to be unconditional if it is to be true, pure love. There are no conditions involved. No strings attached. No, I love you for what you can do for me. A love relationship that is based on expectations can never be pure love from the spiritual realm, but instead is ego self-love.

Michael A. Singer (2007) explains that *"Love is an inner force which is not to be erroneously tied to any one individual. If love is truly pure, it will automatically share itself, unconditionally and non-possessively with all individuals."*

We are not talking about sexual love here, but about love, peace, contentment, security, caring, and protecting. These are all inner forces. Seek them from within, from your fourth chakra, the heart chakra. Do not tolerate love that is offered with behavioral rules for you to follow, for that is not true, pure love. Focus on giving your love to others simply because you want to love them whether they do anything for you or not.

Hopefully, you already had unconditional love for your loved one who is taking you through your anticipatory grief. This time is ideal for practicing true, pure love for another and for yourself. Unconditional love is kind, warm, and tender and not a love that comes and goes. It is continuous over time. It takes all the Elements of Love and rolls them into one. It is known as affection without any limitations, or love without conditions. This term is sometimes associated with other terms such as true altruism or complete love.

Every area of expertise has a certain way of describing unconditional love, but most will agree that it is that type of love which has no boundaries and is unchanging. It is a concept comparable to true love, a term which is generally used to describe the love between lovers. Unconditional love is also used to describe the love between family members, comrades in arms and between others in highly committed relationships. An example of this is a parent's love for their child; no matter a test score, a life-changing decision, an argument, or a strong belief, the amount of love that remains between this bond is seen as unchanging and unconditional. It is caring about the happiness of another person without any thought for what we might get for ourselves.

The ancient Greeks considered the types of love that exist and defined four variations. Of the four, the term agape most closely equates to unconditional love. Agape love is a choice, a decision made to love regardless of circumstances or disappointments. Thus, unconditional love means loving another in their essence, as they are, no matter what they do or fail to do. People with children usually seem to understand this notion best of all. They make the decision to love the child regardless of circumstances. Those caring for a loved one that is dying also can understand this concept. You must choose to love unconditionally. It is learned when practiced over and over again.

Realize that unconditional love is not being "blinded" by love. A person who has newly fallen in love with another is often in this state, where they don't see the other person's full reality or faults. Such a state of love is generally temporary and needs to be replaced by a longer-term, "eyes wide open" type of love in order for the love to last. To love someone without conditions you need to be aware of the conditions, good and bad. Unconditional love is not the case of being blinded by love but rather the resolution that nothing is more important than love itself.

Love is not the same thing as a relationship. Relationships are conditional, a "working partnership." An unconditional relationship is a recipe for one-sided domination. Thus, a relationship can end because the partnership does not function properly, and yet unconditional love toward the other person can remain. Sometimes ending a relationship can be the way to love unconditionally.

Think of unconditional love as an action more than a feeling. We usually consider love to be a feeling, but feelings are a response to something we "get" from someone or something. Therefore, feelings are conditional. Unconditional love is the action, the choice to strive for the well-being of another. The feeling you derive from acting with love is your reward, the return you "get" from your own action.

To love unconditionally is to act with love under all conditions. If you have to do something, or be a certain way, in order to receive love, then that love is conditional. If it is given to you freely and without reservation, it is unconditional.

Love yourself unconditionally. Unconditional love starts at home, with oneself. You know your own flaws and shortcomings better than anyone else, and better than you can ever know anyone else's. Being able to love yourself despite this unsurpassable awareness of your own faults puts you in the position to be able to offer the same to others. Thus, you must be able to recognize, accept, and forgive your own imperfections in order to do the same for someone else. If you cannot deem yourself worthy of being loved unconditionally, you'll never truly be able to deem yourself worthy of offering it.

Make a loving choice. Always ask yourself, "What is the most loving thing I can do for this particular person in this particular moment? Love isn't one size fits all; what might be a loving act toward one person could be harmful to another person, in that it doesn't help them get closer to becoming a truly happy human being. Unconditional love is a new decision you need to make in every situation, not a hard and fast rule you can apply to everyone all the time. For instance, if you have two friends dealing with the loss of a loved one, being the shoulder to cry on and engaging in long talks may be the loving choice for one, while granting some distance and silence may be so for the other.

Forgive those you love. Don't demand or even expect an apology. It's inherently loving to both them and yourself to let go of your anger and resentment toward them. Keep in mind that forgiving is not something we do, but something we are. It is how others talk about us, describe us to the world, such as, "She is a very forgiving person."

In religious terms, you'll hear the phrase "hate the sin, love the sinner." Loving someone unconditionally does not mean liking every action they take or choice they make; it means not letting such things interfere with your desire for the best for that person in all things. If someone you love says something hurtful in anger, the loving choice is usually to help them to know that they are loved. Don't mistake being willing to forgive for letting people walk all over you. Extricating yourself from an environment in which you are repeatedly mistreated or taken advantage of can be a loving choice for both yourself and the other person.

Also, don't expect to shield someone you love from all discomfort and pain. Part of loving someone is fostering their growth as a person, and pain and discomfort are an inescapable part of your growth in this life. Unconditional love means doing what you can to make the other person happy and comfortable, but also helping them grow through their inevitable experiences of discomfort. Don't lie to protect the feelings of someone you love; support them in dealing with their feelings in the face of pain. For example, lying about a dire financial situation to spare pain is likely to foster more pain and distrust in the long run. Instead, be honest, supportive, and eager to work together to find solutions, while giving them unconditional love.

Love more by caring less. But, isn't caring what love is all about? Yes, you want to care for a person in the sense that you strive for their well-being and happiness. You don't want to care in the sense that your love is predicated on specific outcomes, which by definition is conditional. So, not "I don't care what you decide because your well-being is irrelevant to me;" but instead "I don't care what you decide because I just love you regardless of your choices and actions." You don't love in return for actions that make you happy; you derive happiness from the act of loving unconditionally.

Accept yourself and those you love as is. You are far from perfect, and yet you are perfectly capable of offering love. They are likewise imperfect, but worthy of being offered love. Unconditional love is about acceptance—not about expecting others to make you happy through their choices and how they live. You can't control others, only yourself. Your brother may be notorious for his bad choices, but that should have no bearing upon your love for him. Don't love because of how someone lives, but simply because they live.

Go to your journal and make this chapter come alive as part of your life.

Exercises for Chapter 18

1. Make a list of the names of those that you love unconditionally. It should start with your name.

2. Write a paragraph about yourself including why and how you love yourself unconditionally.

3. Choose one name and list why and how you love them unconditionally.

4. Do more names if time permits.

19
Service to Others

What brings you closer to God is being in service to others. I think any religion or spiritual way of life will indicate that service to others will lead to a connection with a higher power.

Steve-O

Service to others is the last Element of Love that we will cover in this book. But, as mentioned before, there are other Elements of Love not covered here. As we live out our lives, fulfilling our plan for our life on earth, and spend time becoming more spiritual, we can see that there are many paths to grow more spiritual, more enlightened. Some paths involve breathing and posture techniques and others that involve disciplining our will. There are paths that train the mind through meditation. There is a path of devotion and one of willful action. Another major opportunity for spiritual growth exists; it is the path of enlightenment through service to others.

The service of caregiving for a loved one that is dying is one way to do service to others. During this time of anticipatory grief, if a person focuses on growing spiritually, much can be accomplished in the level of their own spiritual life. There are so many chances to practice compassion, mercy, and love which take us to a new spiritual level that will last us the rest of our lives and help us in all of our relationships and endeavors.

When we are serving others, we are serving God. It brings us closer to God. Colossians 3:23-24 says, *"Whatever you do, work at it with all your heart as working for the Lord and not for men. It is the Lord you are serving."* Think about helping someone out, and then ask yourself who are you really doing it for? You're doing it for God if you are doing it in an unselfish way, and not expecting any reward or gain for yourself. Matthew 25:40 states that Jesus said, *"What you have done for the humblest of My brothers you have done for Me."* He states it positively, *"If you feed and clothe others, then you feed and clothe Me. If you haven't fed and clothed others, you haven't fed and clothed Me."* The greatest honor is to serve the Lord. By serving people, you are bettering your own character and the character of those around you; one act of kindness leads to another one. It is as contagious as a smile.

Service to others is a learned skill. It comes naturally to some, but others must work at pushing the ego back and pushing God forward. Give of your talents, time and money to others willingly. Share... yes, sharing is one of the first things we learn to do as toddlers. It only grows from there. Service to others is an outward showing of our internal spiritual state of being. Unselfishly sharing ourselves with others is truly an act of love.

Service to others brings us peace as we realize we just made someone else's life a little bit better. If you are the caregiver to the person dying, you are certainly giving service to that person. There is so much to gain in this situation for it is hard in many ways but when grieving is over, you will have peace knowing you shared yourself and made their life better than it might have been.

If you work in a nursing home, you live a part of your life in the period of anticipatory grieving on a daily basis. You may not have the emotional attachment that you could have with a loved one, but still, as nurses, we all have favorite patients and feel much of the same emotions. Know that you are spiritually giving service to others and allow that thought to give you peace. You are growing spiritually, and your soul is growing too.

A quote from Buddha says, *"If you light a lamp for someone else it will also brighten your path."*

Service to others requires us to put our needs aside and do something for another human being without any thought of, desire for, or expectation of something being done for us in return. It requires unselfishness on our part. It opens the door to our heart and allows our love to spread to those around us. Giving up something that you wanted to do so that you can do something for another or being willing to schedule doing something for another is a way of growing more spiritual. Others will see your example and feel your love, which in turn is God's love.

Again, the ego must be conquered and pushed back. For service to others to lead you to spiritual growth, it must be done with no thought of grandiose of self. It must be done just because someone needs help and you have a desire to lend a hand. Don't allow yourself to be used, abused, or taken advantage of in these situations.

Opportunities to give service to others during anticipatory grieving are abundant. Offering to take a person to their doctor's appointment or any appointment can be such a blessing to the persons in need. Something as simple as taking them shopping or taking a list to the store to pick up the groceries for them is another example. Cleaning the floors in their home is a very difficult thing for someone who is not feeling well and if you are able to do this for someone, it will be appreciated. Your love for others will show and you will feel love come back to you as well.

I have included a poem that explains how service to others helps us to know God better.

Unawares

They said, "The Master is coming
To honor the town to-day,
And none can tell at what house or home
The Master will choose to stay."

And I thought while my heart beat wildly,
What if He should come to mine,
How would I strive to entertain
And honor the Guest Divine!

And straight I turned to toiling
To make my house more neat;
I swept, and polished, and garnished.
And decked it with blossoms sweet.

I was troubled for fear the Master
Might come ere my work was done,
And I hasted and worked the faster,
And watched the hurrying sun.

But right in the midst of my duties
A woman came to my door;
She had come to tell me her sorrows
And my comfort and aid to implore,

And I said, "I cannot listen
Nor help you any, to-day;
I have greater things to attend to."
And the pleader turned away.

But soon there came another-
A cripple, thin, pale and gray-
And said, "Oh, let me stop and rest
A while in your house, I pray!

I have traveled far since morning,
I am hungry, and faint, and weak;
My heart is full of misery,
And comfort and help I seek."

And I cried, "I am grieved and sorry,
But I cannot help you to-day.
I look for a great and noble Guest,"
And the cripple went away;

And the day wore onward swiftly-
And my task was nearly done,
And a prayer was ever in my heart
That the Master to me might come.

And I thought I would spring to meet Him,
And serve him with utmost care,
When a little child stood by me
With a face so sweet and fair-

Sweet, but with marks of teardrops-
And his clothes were tattered and old;
A finger was bruised and bleeding,
And his little bare feet were cold.

And I said, "I'm sorry for you-
You are sorely in need of care;
But I cannot stop to give it,
You must hasten other where."

And at the words, a shadow
Swept o'er his blue-veined brow, -
"Someone will feed and clothe you, dear,
But I am too busy now."

At last the day was ended,
And my toil was over and done;
My house was swept and garnished-
And I watched in the dark-alone.

Watched-but no footfall sounded,
No one paused at my gate;
No one entered my cottage door;
I could only pray-and wait.

I waited till night had deepened,
And the Master had not come.
"He has entered some other door," I said,
"And gladdened some other home!"

My labor had been for nothing,
And I bowed my head and I wept,
My heart was sore with longing-
Yet-in spite of it all-I slept.

Then the Master stood before me,
And his face was grave and fair;
"Three times to-day I came to your door,
And craved your pity and care;

Three times you sent me onward,
Unhelped and uncomforted;
And the blessing you might have had was lost,
And your chance to serve has fled."

> "O Lord, dear Lord, forgive me!
> How could I know it was Thee?"
> My very soul was shamed and bowed
> In the depths of humility.
>
> And He said, "The sin is pardoned,
> But the blessing is lost to thee;
> You have failed to comfort Me.
> For comforting not, the least of Mine!"
>
> Emma A. Lent

To serve others is to minister to others and help them in various ways. Do not do it for show or publicity, but simply to enrich and help the lives of others and in doing so, enrich your own life as well. Everyone can help others in some form or another and can realize that helping others can give our lives a sense of meaning and purpose. Mother Teresa is a good example because she dedicated her life to serving others and found a deep sense of fulfillment. This feeling of fulfillment can be yours to experience as well when you serve others.

You can achieve almost anything you want to achieve, if you believe in yourself and put your heart and mind to it. This level of self-belief allows you to know that you will be okay, no matter what happens. God is always at your side. Serving people is easy when we know who we are and what we are about. Many believe that our true purpose in life is to spend it giving to others—that we receive happiness, fulfillment, and meaning in return.

Many believe we should all contribute to the welfare of others by helping meet physical, emotional, and spiritual needs whenever we can. The Bible tells us that Jesus came into this world to serve others, not to be served. Serving others might be considered as work by some but is an act of worship and spiritual activity. Jesus was a servant and showed us how to serve others with forgiveness. Look for ways to help others, to give, and to build others up. Jesus was giving his disciples an example when he washed their feet before the Last Supper. As a Christian, God calls you to be ministers and have a heart to serve others and put the needs of others above our own. This is spoken about in other religions as well.

All of the Elements of Love listed in Part 3 are tickets to your spiritual growth. It is all so simple. Love God, love yourself, love others and practice, practice, practice.

Explore your own service to others in your life by turning to the exercises on the next page.

Exercises for Chapter 19

1. List what you have done for someone else in the past week. If you can't think of something in that time frame, then go back as far as you need to go to remember when you last did something for someone else, with no thought of recognition or self-pride.

2. Plan to be alert to opportunities to help others. During anticipatory grief, there are many opportunities. Keep a journal for the next week or even a month to prove to yourself that you do help others.

3. Plan to do random acts of kindness in the future. This is a service to others as well.

PART 4

Elements of Successful Spiritual Growth

Introduction to Part 4
Elements of Successful Spiritual Growth

The information in Part Four will help you to write a plan and then follow through to become more spiritual throughout the rest of your life if you continue to practice what you have learned so far. You will know God better and have a closer walk with Him. You will have wonderful relationships and be happier—more than you could have ever imagined. You will have less depression, less hurt, less anxiety and you will be described by others as more loving and forgiving. You will be successful in your spiritual growth and you will know it! There will be no doubt in your mind. Others will see it as well. You will be a changed person. This change, this knowledge, will stay with you for the rest of your life.

20
Successful Spiritual Growth

Progress is impossible without change, and those who cannot change their minds cannot change anything.
George Bernard Shaw

For complete success in growing spiritually you must have a plan. Without a plan you will get stuck, confused and perhaps stop trying to change yourself. You will continue to be the same as you are now without experiencing the spiritual growth, God's love, and the glorious peace that you could have. At the very least, without a plan, it will take you longer to feel any accomplishment.

First and foremost, you must decide that you want to grow spiritually. You must be willing to embrace change in yourself, in the way you think, the way you act and respond. In time, others around you will see the difference and in fact, start mirroring your new, more loving ways. Love is contagious. To grow spiritually, is to expand your love to others and to yourself. Prayerfully ask that the change that you want to make is to serve God, then He will invoke spiritual forces to support you in your effort.

Remember, during the time of anticipatory grieving we are learning lessons that we planned to experience before our birth. We planned this time, this experience, so we would learn something special, something specific to our soul's needs. Our loved one also planned it to experience and learn things that are specific to their soul's needs as well. To begin, consider your own objectives. Then empower those objectives by taking a moment to make a deliberate choice about what you hope to experience and achieve.

It is important to remember that a difficult phase doesn't end until our lessons are learned. We will continue to experience difficult times until all lessons have been satisfied to our soul's needs. Anticipatory grief is a difficult time unless we choose to make it a period of special learning. Growing spiritually is the answer. Sit down and write out a plan. It can be simple, but I can guarantee you that as you start working on accomplishing this plan, you will grow in an abundance of understanding that God and His universe will send your way.

There will be in between times where you will no longer be who you used to be but haven't arrived to be who you want to be yet. It is like changing clothes. One second you are dressed and then you are naked for a minute before putting on a new set of clothes. Spiritual in the present moment, our task is to let go of what we are, with love and sometimes sorrow, and embrace what emerges next from the spiritual realm to help us to become who we really are.

You may feel that you do not know how to get started. If you are already familiar with God through your own way, or the way of your church, just build on it. See your pastor or spiritual advisor. You can see a professional intuitive (psychic) that has good references. God has unconditional love for all ways that have love as the basis of faith and action. If you don't have a pastor, visit with a spiritual advisor that has been recommended by someone that you trust. It can be a lay person that has traveled this road before, and you admire how they have grown in spirituality themselves.

There are many spiritual authors that can give you guidance on how to plan, especially if this spirituality stuff is all new to you. Sanaya Roman has written many books on this subject. The best one is called *"Spiritual Growth."* Linda Howe's book *"Discover Soul's Path Through the Akashic Records,"* has an excellent plan to adopt. She uses the outline of "Awareness, Acceptance, Appreciation," and last but not least, "Appropriate Action." Read her book for the details. Deepak Chopra, Marianne Williamson, and many more writers want to help you. If you feel most comfortable with Zen teachings, author, Thich Nhat Hauh, is a good one to explore. You just need to get started.

The most read book on Earth is the Bible. Look to the Bible if you receive helpful messages from it. Some claim that although it is a good book, they just don't always understand what some of the verses are meaning. They seem to need a more detailed message that speaks to them. They are not blaming the Bible, but instead their own inability to relate to the verbiage used.

I would suggest that you use a very simple method and one that always works. Have a talk with God. That always works and helps you to learn how to listen to God. Ask Him to guide you. This can be done through prayer followed up with daily meditation. Meditation is the key to keeping you on track, no matter which method you choose to use as your plan to grow more spiritual. Meditation quiets our busy mind and we can listen for directions. After meditation you can document the parts of your plan of which you received help. If it is not written down in your journal, you are apt to forget or at the very least, you may get mixed up. Writing what you received in meditation will help you turn it into a plan. Sometimes nothing comes through in meditation but wait and listen because God will show you the way. You can call upon your Angels; they want to help you, too.

Allow God to lead you. Believe that He will. Watch carefully for signs of God working in your life, helping you to stay on track. Your answers may not come while you are meditating, but later, sometimes days later. It could come while reading when in that holy instant you "know" God put that information in front of you to notice. It could come in the words of a song, poem, or something you heard on TV, radio or in the movies. God is all around you and is in everything as well.

Use affirmations to help remind you that you are on a special mission. That mission is to become more spiritual and in doing so, you will have a happier life. Affirmations are positive statements that give us a way to remember to stay positive each time we see or say them. Tape them to your bathroom mirror, or inside (or outside) your kitchen cabinets or workspace of your choice. They serve to remind you of your mission during this period of grieving. Repetition of affirmations are helpful; they will deepen your current level of comprehension and strengthen your skills.

Ask God to send you new acquaintances that are in a similar situation. This goes for not only others in an anticipatory grieving situation but more importantly new friends or rekindle old relationships with others that know they are on a spiritual journey too. There are all levels of knowledge in those around us. Tap into that knowledge base to build on yours. Stay as yourself. Be who you are meant to be. Don't allow others to continue to influence you if you are uncomfortable with their beliefs. Be certain that their way sounds like truth to you. It is okay to go slow and check often with yourself to see if you can truly believe what they are advocating. If not, take what feels like truth to you and leave the rest behind. That goes for this book as well. Be who you are!

Be careful to not judge the other person if you don't buy into what they believe. They have their path and you have yours. They are where they are supposed to be, and it is just not where you are supposed to be at this time. Let it be.

Spiritual growth comes in a series of small revelations over time. Yes, there can be some really big ones, but most come to us as ideas in understandings, clarifications, and are subtle in nature. They are the teachings of God and His universe. They come when we are open to receive, when we are in need to know or need to understand something better. They come when we are at a higher vibration and not in fear of receiving from God and the spiritual realm.

Michael A. Singer (2007) explains it this way, *"The spiritual journey is one of constant transformation. In order to grow, you must give up the struggle to remain the same, and learn to embrace change at all times. Real transformation comes when you embrace your problems as agents for growth."*

Witness your problem and then let it go. You are aware of the drama, but you don't engage and become consumed in the drama. This makes you free. When you are no longer absorbed in your own drama, but instead sit comfortably deep inside the seat of awareness, that area deep within, you will start to feel this flow of energy coming up from deep within. This is God, this is Spirit filling you with love and contentment.

Singer continues, *"Awareness does not fight; awareness releases."* Don't take the issues on as a battle. Just be aware and see it as none of your business. The universe is working on it on your behalf. This is the essence of a spiritual life. Once you learn that it is okay to feel inner disturbances and that they can no longer disturb your seat of inner consciousness, you will be free. You will know you are growing spiritually. Once you taste this freedom, this ecstasy, you will want to experience this inner flow again and again. The freedom it brings will sustain you and protect you from the world's problems, as well as your own problems. Do what you must regarding the problem and then let it go. Visit this inner sanctuary daily. Be aware of any directions given to you from Spirit. Use awareness instead of worry or trying to control everything. This is how you grow in spirituality. This is how you become free.

There are many opportunities during this block of time to practice this. When you have the knowledge that you are on a spiritual path anyway, as you are and everybody else is too, then using this seemingly stressful time of sadness and grief is the answer to make it become something wonderful to help you and your loved one. What you learn and change in yourself can be there for the rest of your life. Other relationships will be enhanced as well. You will be more pleasant to be around because you are concerned with harmony, not controlling everything. You will be free to love and be loved back. So be aware, yet not immersed in every disturbance. Use this time to grow spiritually. See it as a blessing and a beautiful gift to have more time with your loved one.

Learn to be more spontaneous to grow in your comfort level of not being able to wrap up all the details of your life. Learn to live by the inner light. The inner light eliminates stress and anger. The inner light helps you to grow spiritually. Will you always be able to stay on top? No, of course not. But you will recover more quickly because you will have such good support from the universe to do so.

Plan how you will get in contact with God on a daily basis. Meditation will probably work best. Daily devotions may work for you if you are listening to God's message through the devotion for that day. Strike out on your own and just have a conversation with God and ask how He wants you to do this. Look for classes in your town. Metaphysical bookstores are a good choice to research for classes. Your church may have classes. Groups can be good but if groups aren't possible or you don't like groups, then look online for information and classes. You don't really need classes if you have a good connection with God, but they can be helpful to observe how God has worked with others. Meet new people that may be exploring the same topics as you. Look for a spiritual coach. There is a myriad of ways to explore and grow.

Use the list of the Elements of Love in Part Three to get started with your plan. Choose one or two to work on first. Use your journal to write your plan down. How much time will you spend doing what you feel led to do? How will you measure yourself? Plan in as much detail as you can at first and then let God and His universe help you along the way. Opportunities that you didn't think of will be presented in your path as you work on say, compassion. Be alert to noticing these opportunities and think about how you did as you realized it was an opportunity to be compassionate. What will you do next time you are presented with this opportunity? Don't forget to practice. That is how you will get good at it and grow spiritually.

Be sure to date the notes in your journal as to what messages you received, what occurrences were put in your path and how you dealt with them. Analyze how you handled the situation and whether or not you could have done it differently. Be kind to yourself. Give yourself praise when it is earned and don't be overly concerned if you didn't do it as well as you intended. Remember, "mistakes make masters." Hopefully you learned what to do differently next time. And when it is important to our spiritual growth, God will see that the situation comes up again and again until we grow into getting it right.

God is not disappointed and will not punish us when we mess up. He loves us and knows that when we didn't quite get it right, we still learned more about how to get it right next time. God loves us and He will be there to help us. He provided Angels, Ascended Masters, Spirit Guides, and other entities to help us from the spirit world. He will provide other humans to step into our life when we need them. People come into our lives for a reason, a season, or for a lifetime. This time frame of anticipatory grief enables us to meet new people at times and those persons in our life can be there for a reason, season or perhaps that person that we get to know better becomes a special person for the rest of our life.

Get started today. The love, contentment, and joy for your life will make it all worth it when you see that you are growing and providing harmony in your midst instead of judgement, anger, and pain. None of us need the drama that society seems to like and encourage on social media. You will want to put your phone down, turn it off, or at least put it where you can't hear it during your meditation time and experience the miracle of silence. Remember the song.... Silence is Golden? It truly is.

Go back into the other chapters in this book as well to decide what to put in your plan. For example, the chapters on Ego and Fear are so important. We must master the ego and our fears if we want to grow spiritually. Be sure to include how to master them as part of your plan. Decide now what you need most so you can get started and then your plan can grow over time.

Before this chapter comes to an end, I want to share Sanaya Roman's (1989) list of the rewards of living a spiritual life:

- *You release old programming that no longer serves you*
- *Supportive, positive people are drawn into your life*
- *You empower yourself and others in all you do and say*
- *You know who you are, why you are here, and what your higher purpose is*
- *Lifestyle and environment support your life purpose and greater work in the world*
- *You explore new possibilities and choices and continually expand your vision of what is possible*

- *Have tools to draw to yourself the opportunities, people, and events you need to create your life's work*
- *Operate from your heart and trust your inner messages and take action upon them*
- *Conscious of energy around you and the effects other people have upon it*
- *You are present in the moment, alert, aware, and at a high level of observation all the time*
- *You spark growth in others*
- *You create change by working the highest spiritual level rather than working at the personality level*
- *A clearer sense of direction, a greater feeling of being in control*
- *A deeper understanding of why things are happening*
- *Increasing calmness and a life that is joyful and loving to yourself*

Go to your journal now and get stated planning how you will grow more spiritual.

Bless You! Namaste!

Exercises for Chapter 20

1. After giving it some thought, write a plan to help you through this period of anticipatory grieving. Start with the decision to become more spiritual. How do you feel about your situation and of living through this stressful time? What do you want to improve? What or who will your obstacles be? Who is already in your life that will help you? Who are you comfortable enough with to talk to about your desire to be more spiritual? Look at your notes from the previous chapters. How can you incorporate this into your plan?

2. 2. How you will measure yourself? How you will know you have grown? Will it be how others react to you differently? Will it be how you feel about yourself, your life? Will it be that you are happier, more content, more loving, less angry?

3. Know that your plan will change over time. Leave room in your mind to be open to change at any moment. Allow yourself to go to the next step as you mature in knowledge and love. Know that there really is no ending whereby you feel you have arrived and can stop growing spiritually. This will become your life's work. It will feel glorious!

PART 5

My Stories

Introduction to Part 5
My Story

Although I invited others to share their experiences with anticipatory grief, no one took the offer except for the poems that have been shared in this book. My anticipatory grief story starts in the early 1990s when my husband started on a long journey, which included many poor health issues over time. We married on July 26, 1958 and have had a wonderful life together. As of the writing of this book, we just celebrated our 60th Wedding Anniversary. Never in my wildest dreams did I ever think that we would see our 60th anniversary. We have been so blessed and I thank God for all the wonderful things that we have experienced together.

There are two stories for Part 5. The first story is about our family pet, a dog named Deacon. The second story is about my husband, Norm.

21
Deacon

*If you have a dog, you most likely outlive it.
To get a dog is to open yourself to profound joy
and, prospectively, to equally profound sadness.*
Marjorie Garber

    The day came when I was confronted with a terrible responsibility. I knew it was coming and I didn't want to face it. I had to make the decision when the right time to put our beloved pet dog down would be. It happened just before this book went to the publisher. This story is included because it mirrors the message in this book. We can have anticipatory grief for anything that we love, and that we know we will have to give up some day. For me, in this case it was a beloved pet, but it could be something else for you.

    It was right after Thanksgiving of 2018 when his health condition worsened, and I knew it was time for him to go. Life on Earth had gotten to be too much for him. Thankfully we can help our animal loved ones to not suffer any longer than necessary. Yes, it is hard to make the decision, but it must be made out of love for them, and not out of our own selfish desire to keep them alive and with us as long as they are breathing which can cause them to suffer longer just for us. That was exactly one of the problems; he couldn't breathe very well at times. It was like an extended asthma attack. I know it was scary for him and was painful as well. He also had had bloody stools for four years due to a benign tumor in his colon, which was growing and closing off his ability to pass stool. He had allergies, ear problems and cataracts. He had even suffered a stroke on Easter, April 2017, and lived to recover 100%.

Our beloved pet was a Jack Russell Terrier named Deacon. Deacon was the best pet ever for us. We called ourselves Grandma and Grandpa to him when we got him, and it stuck for his entire life. That was how he knew us. You see, we were grandparents when we got him and didn't want to go back to Mama and Daddy titles.

Deacon was five weeks old when we got him, and lived to be fifteen years old, so we had been together for a long time. In doggie years, he was the equivalent of 105 years old. He looked old and acted old much of the time. About once a week he would manage to do a power run around the house after being outside to potty. Jack Russell's love those power runs! I cherish those years now more than ever. Our hearts are breaking as we adjust to not having him around.

His energy is imprinted everywhere around our house, car and yard. I see him everywhere as I go about my day. I had not realized just how much of our lives had been devoted to making his life better. He was a happy little guy and seemed to enjoy life. He was as devoted to taking care of us as we were in taking care of him.

Deacon was especially sick the Saturday after Thanksgiving that led me to make my decision during mediation on Sunday morning. I later talked it over with Norm and he reluctantly agreed. Norm did not want to be in the room when it happened, but I did. I knew that Deacon would be scared, and I wanted to comfort him. I called the vet on Monday morning and took the 12-noon appointment that was offered. I gave him his anti-anxiety medicine at 10:15am, an hour before we left for town. Deacon was a little drowsy and I let him ride to town on my lap instead of being tethered in his usual perch between the two front seats in the truck. I needed to hold him, hug him and give him love. All the way to town I was thinking, he is so precious and has been such a good companion for all these fifteen years.

We arrived at the vet's office a little early but sat in the car while Norm said his good-byes to Deacon. I really do believe that Deacon knew what was going to happen and I also know that we were surrounded by loving spiritual beings that would help us through this thing that he seemed ready and willing to do. Angel energy was everywhere.

I carried him into the building. They took us right back to a room with subdued lighting and a Disneyland themed pillow bed on the examining table. The lady did what she needed to do paperwork wise and had me sign a consent, then she left us alone for about 10 minutes. Deacon wanted to get down off of the examining table but didn't try too hard. He mostly just nuzzled his face into my chest. It was a time and feeling that I will never forget. I believed he knew what was happening and he was telling me he wished he could be healthy and stay to take care of us forever. Dear God, how I wished it, too.

The doctor came in and explained the procedure to me. He then gave Deacon an injection into his hip that would put him to sleep (a mild anesthesia) and left the room for 10 more minutes. Deacon was still very loving, nuzzling his face into my chest. I will forever cherish that memory and the feeling of love that passed between us as long as I live. He was not scared and was cooperative of all that was asked of him.

I was able to talk with him until he slowly went to sleep. I reassured him that I would not leave him. The doctor came back and softly said I could leave or stay as I wished. They were so professional and caring. I told him I would stay until he was gone... (as I had promised Deacon). Then the vet gave him an IV medicine that ended his life. I stayed until I was sure he was gone.

So, so, so sad! My baby boy was dead! My emotions were so strong with grief yet knowing that we had made the right decision. I just wish it could have been different. We knew when we got him that this day would arrive that we would have to say goodbye. We were lucky, so many pets die much younger.

On the way home I spiritually saw him and felt the presence of his essence. I had told him he could come home with us in his new spiritual body if he wanted to... and he did! At home everywhere I looked, every thought I had was of Deacon. I missed him more than I ever thought I could.

Our daughter-in-law, Kristie at her home in another town, said that she knew what time he had died because all six of their dogs got whiny at 12:20 pm, and then all subdued and quiet at 12:25 pm, the time that the doctor pronounced Deacon dead. Apparently, Deacon had visited them in spirit at that time as these were his buddies and he would want to say good-bye to them.

Here at home, I continued to feel his essence, as well as the essence of Snoopy, another Jack Russell Terrier that belonged to our son, but lived with us for

Deacon's first year of life. Snoopy taught him all the tricks, so to speak, some of which could have been left out. Deacon would copy everything that Snoopy did. Sadly, Snoopy passed away about five years before Deacon. I do believe Snoopy came to escort Deacon to his Heavenly home. Through my tears, I could spiritually see Deacon walking up to Snoopy and doing the little hip swing that he always did, bumping into Snoopy's side to get him to play with him. Somehow it was comforting for me to know that he was not alone, but with an old friend and playing again. Watch out Angels... Snoopy and Deacon might do a dueling power run all over Heaven!

Many tears, many memories, many heartaches have happened since that day as we try to adjust to life without him. He was special, so special. We have had so much more emotion, heartache and tears over Deacon these past few days. I didn't expect the depth or the magnitude of what we were experiencing. I suppose there will be many more days before we are able to talk about him without tears. It has helped to put his picture next to where Norm sits so we can look at it from time to time. It just makes us feel better. We feel like we have lost one of our children and we do know how that feels because we experienced that loss when our daughter passed away in 1967.

I know we did the right thing for Deacon. He was hurting, scared and was sleeping most of the daytime. He couldn't stand to be away from Norm, his Grandpa. He was Grandpa's dog, but I know he loved me too. He started taking more care of me after I was in a car accident in September of 2017.

Deacon took his job to care for us very seriously. He believed he had to keep track of us around the house or yard. One thing he took upon himself, as his job, was making sure that Norm came to the table to eat. As soon as he saw me start to cook or set the table, he decided that it was time for Grandpa to come to the table, so he would run up to Norm's chair and start barking for him to come to the table. It was his job. Jack Russell Terriers love to have a job.

When he was just a few weeks old, Deacon started riding in a box on Grandpa's ATV. He loved the ATV rides with Grandpa. This was exciting to him his entire life. If there was another ATV along on the trip, he insisted on being the leader of the pack. He also didn't like it when Norm would put the ATV in reverse. He would turn around and bark at Grandpa, as if telling him that he was going the wrong way. Deacon kept a close watch on each movement that Norm made as he started the ATV. We joked that if he had thumbs, he would be able to drive it himself.

Although Deacon loved humans, he wanted to be the only dog in the room. He would tolerate the other visiting dogs if they would leave him alone, but if they got too close and smelled his bottom, he would nip at them! I've seen very large Labradors make a wide circle around him to avoid being nipped at. They knew without a doubt that this was his territory. He served as a wonderful doorbell to alert us of the arrival of our company. When they were seated and things settled down from their arrival, he would sit very near the company, usually on their feet. He was even a good mouser, until a couple of years ago when a mouse bit him on the lip. No more mice for him!

Yes, I experienced anticipatory grief for Deacon, for at least four years. It has now ended, and

I find myself going through the five steps of grieving, as I have now entered the type of grief that comes after death. They are different, very different.

Rest in peace, Dear Deacon. We will all be together again someday in our Heavenly home.

22
My Experience

All you need to be on a truly spiritual path
Is to constantly and consciously
choose LOVE.
Eckhart Tolle

As I was writing this book, I was constantly evaluating my own situation. Currently, I am living this experience of anticipatory grief as I go through the sorrow of waiting for a loved one to die. I'm sure my situation is no different than many others that read this book.

I have been here before. Not only now with my husband, Norm and until very recently, our precious family dog, a Jack Russell named Deacon, whom you just read about in the previous chapter, but also with my mother and stepdad, and my father and stepmom. They each gave me spans of time to explore and grow from by experiencing the grief that comes before the actual passing of a loved one. I have also experienced the sudden passing of my little girl, Kathy. She passed during her fourth year on earth in 1967. Her passing was quite fast and unexpected and did not qualify to be called anticipatory grieving. From personal experience, I can tell you that losing one of your children is the greatest grief of all. So, I understand grief on all levels of the term grief.

Returning to my current story of anticipatory grief, I love my husband, and he loves me. I don't want him to die. He doesn't want to die. I want him to recover so we can get back to living life as we did before. But of course, I know that will not happen…not this time. We have been married for 60 years as of July 26, 2018. We have built a life together having three children, nine grandchildren and eighteen great-grandchildren. We have many extended family and friends as well.

In 1973, we bought his family ranch in North Idaho where he grew up. With the help of our two sons, we built a log home on it for us, using logs from the property. This was a dream he had had for many years. My husband loves this land with all of his heart and soul. He doesn't want to leave it. He loves the wildlife that live on this property. We look out our windows and enjoy a group of deer eating the grass in our expansive back yard, or a moose walking down the driveway, ducking its head to see in our front windows. It is like no other place on this side of Heaven.

As time progressed, his health deteriorated, and he decided to retire in 1996. Then later, when he could no longer hunt and work on our acreage, he discovered a wonderful hobby that involves trail cameras that he can continue to do even now.

Norm currently has a great number of cameras strategically placed on our 80 acres, and he often rides his four-wheeler (the only way he can go as he can't walk very far) to retrieve the SD cards and replace them with new cards. The retrieved SD cards are so much fun for him to download to the computer after he returns home. He has seen wildlife that others could only dream of having in their yards, even more than when he was a kid growing up in these woods. Besides the deer, we have trail cam pictures of elk, moose, bobcat, cougar, wild turkeys, grouse, raccoon and bear. He even has pictures of a fisher cat, which is pretty rare here. The resident beaver made a lake in the center of our property and it is a draw to so many of nature's wildlife including waterfowl. Eagles fly over our house quite often. We see the babies of the wildlife year after year and we marvel at how many years this has gone on for us. We have been so blessed by God to have been able to live here for so long. It has been thirty-three years and counting living on this property.

In the past there have been many episodes of life-threatening illnesses for my husband, most of them he has recovered from and gone on to live a reasonably healthy life. But not this time. I know it; he knows it, too. There is rarely any talk about his pending death. He doesn't seem to believe he will really die, not soon any way. So, we never talk about what I will do after his death. I have planned on my own to a point, so that I will not be caught off guard when I find myself alone and on my own. We are so blessed because we have a good support team in place with such a large loving family nearby as well as many, many friends going out of their way to help.

His illnesses started with Colon Cancer in the early 1990s, while he was in his fifties. In time, he became a cancer survivor. He has suffered arthritis, high blood pressure, pulmonary hypertension, enlarged heart, and Cardiac Sick Sinus Syndrome leading to the need for a cardiac pacemaker in 2011. All of these chronic conditions came on during about a ten-year period and never really ever went away. Other, less life-threatening, conditions came on as well, seemingly one on top of another. For example, he had many surgeries for joint replacements in both knees in the mid-1990s and a shoulder joint replacement in 2005. During that surgery, he had a near death experience in the operating room. He also had a scary congestive heart failure episode in the fall of 2005 and has suffered many episodes of diverticulitis and gall bladder problems. These have continued for the rest of his life to date, because he refuses surgery. He is on oxygen 24/7 and has little energy to do so many of the things that he loved to do. He walks with a cane due to the advanced arthritis, and he continues to have a heart condition that occasionally gives him a cardiac arrhythmia — which can cause sudden death, if it persists too long.

Throughout most of these illnesses, my husband has maintained as normal a life as possible. He has a huge ability to persevere through anything it seems. He has mostly denied his health issues as something that will cause him to slow down, that is, until the last few years when even he could not deny that his physical body is beginning to give out. And yet, his mind and brain has stayed alert. For that, of course, we are so thankful.

Therefore, my own experience is truly one of anticipatory grieving, which has gone on, at least on and off, for twenty-five to thirty years. I had to find a way to get through it the best way I could. Focusing on growing spiritually was the way for me. I decided to write a book so that I could share my experience with others. As you reflect back on what you have read in this book, I want you to know that I have experienced everything I have written about. As I wrote on a topic, I experienced it. God said to me, "If you are asking this of others, you should experience it yourself." And experience it I did — some of it over and over again and am continuing to do so. I know I'm asking something of you that is hard... but it is do-able because I have done it.

I know that I have grown more spiritual or I would not have been able to endure the sadness for so long. In fact, my husband and I have grown more spiritual together. Now in these twilight years, I watch him grow kinder as I grow kinder, more loving, more compassionate, more understanding. We are growing closer and more love passes between us as we both grow more spiritual while we are on this journey called life. I hope your grieving journey involving another doesn't last as long as mine has. But I hope you can love in the now and grow closer as you both wait.

It is important to remember that anticipatory grief doesn't have to be something involving an impending death of a loved one. The wait can be for anything that involves grieving a loss. The loss can be a condition that takes a long time to heal or anything that involves being forced to change your life for another or even for yourself. Accepting devastating conditions like paralysis and learning to live life differently is included. The time spent waiting involves a loss of some kind before a new life is able to be undertaken. In every situation, however, growing more spiritual is the answer to all of life's problems.

The most important message in this book is to use these simple spiritual ideas and values to become happier for the rest of your life, regardless of your situation or your religious leanings. Just love God, love mankind, and love yourself while you wait. The practice you get from this wait is making you strong and these things will stay with you and work for you, in all of your relationships for the rest of your life. And the greatest part... You will truly learn to know God at his fullest.

PART 6

Deacon's Story
By
Deacon

Part 6 Introduction

Deacon's Story
By Deacon

Chapters 23 through 27 are dedicated to my husband's and my emotional health in grieving our beloved pet's death. I suggested earlier in the book to do something like this to help you move forward in your own grieving process after the death occurs. Writing this book as though Deacon was the author was insightful, fun, and most of all, very therapeutic for both of us. It helped us to move forward in grieving the loss of Deacon. It helped us realize that we could not have taken better care of him had he been human. We realize that we did a good job in being the stewards of his life. Deacon's ill health for the last four years created a situation of anticipatory grief for us to go through. We loved this little dog; although we know he is happy in Heaven, we miss him terribly.

The time spent writing this book through Deacon's eyes, allowed us to reminisce all the funny, loving times we had with him during the fifteen years that he gave to us. Although all events are true, so many were left out due to spacing. Of course, they will not be forgotten.

Deacon was a very special, very intelligent little dog with a large understanding of vocabulary. We often spelled things so he wouldn't know, but somehow, he always knew anyway.

People may say, "He was only a dog." Yes, he was a dog. However, to us, he was like one of our own children. We suffer the loss just as much. If you feel your pets are like part of the family, then you will understand. Although we love and miss him, we find comfort in publishing his story. It helps us be able to move forward. Thank you for reading it.

23
In The Beginning

Mama told me that it was a warm sunny day in beautiful North Idaho when I was born. In fact, it was July 17, 2003, in Cocolala, Idaho. I knew I had other brothers and sisters because it was a real fight to find and keep a nipple so I could eat. But, when I did get a hold of one, I kept it! It felt so good to be nuzzled up against Mama. She was so warm and loving. I was sure that I was her favorite as she licked me and cared for me.

After my eyes opened, WOW! I was surprised to see that there were six of us that Mama had to care for and feed. I also learned that I had an older sister from a batch of puppies before my batch. Her name was Spin. The lady that owned Mama named her that because when Spin would get excited and happy, she would jump up in the air twirling around mid-air before coming back down. I asked her if she would teach me how to do that and she said she would when I got older. Right now, I just needed to learn to walk right.

One day we were all put into a box and then into the back seat of a car. We traveled to a place that smelled like lots of different dogs and Mama told us that the other smell, the bad one, was from something called "cats." She promised to teach us all about cats someday. But for now, we were going to see a nice man. I later learned that he was a doctor, called a vet or something like that. We had to do this, she said.

Boy! I was first. I guess that was a good thing because I would have been more scared if I had to wait and watch my brothers and sisters get their shots and tails cut shorter. They also cut off one toe on each front leg. I know, it sounds like it would really hurt, but it only stung for a little while. Maybe he did something to make it not hurt. We all survived the visit to the vet. I never want to go back there again. I'll never forget that smell.

A side note here... later when I was older, I heard my humans say that my tail had been cut too short! Jack Russell Terrier's tails were supposed to be long enough to be a handle to help free us from a fox hole. But my humans said they didn't care, they loved me anyway.

I also learned that the history of the breed of Jack Russell Terrier's came into existence in England during the time that fox hunts were popular. The bigger dogs chased the fox and sometimes it would go down into a hole. That was when the Jack Russell Terriers were brought out and encouraged to go into the hole and bring the fox out... unharmed. It was not to be killed ... YET! WOW! That sounds awful for the fox! It must have been really scary to be chased in the first place by a bunch of dogs yelping and barking at you and then when it found some safety in the hole, my ancestors would drag it out and the chase would continue. How awful!

Our chest cavities are very narrow and deep. The cavity can contract smaller, which allows us to go into narrow holes. But sometimes we would get stuck in the hole. A man on the hunt would reach down in the hole and get a grip on the tail of the Jack Russell Terrier and pull it out, fox and all.

I learned that the man that perfected the breed was a Parson in England. His name was Parson Jack

Russell. Fox Terrier and English Walker Hound were the main breeds that ended up producing the Jack Russell Terriers. The original Jack Russell Terriers were 90% white and had long legs and short, straight hair. Their tummies were grizzled (dark spots covering some of the pink).

Later when the fox hunts were outlawed in England and the land became divided up by fences, it was hard for the long-legged ones to get through the fences. Breeders came up with a short-legged version and the hair became different also during the hybrid breeding process. Today there are long-legged and short-legged ones plus three kinds of hair; short, long and broken (tuffs of long hair mixed in with short hair).

I looked like the original Jack Russell Terriers and I was a "sharp looker", if I so say so myself. I was long-legged, more than 90% white with very pretty markings on my face. I had dark outlines around my eyes that made my eyes look like I had eyeliner on. My humans really liked that about me. I don't know what my daddy looked like, I never saw him, but I know Mama was beautiful. I must have taken after her for sure.

One day different humans started coming around looking at us, picking us up and hugging us, talking baby talk. They seemed to like some of us more than others and talked with the lady that owned Mama. They passed green paper back and forth. After the people were gone some of my siblings had a new special collar put on them. I didn't understand why some of us got them and some of us didn't. We were three weeks old.

Then one day a new man and woman came looking at those of us that didn't have a collar yet. The man did most of the looking, the woman seemed to like all of us. They were really nice. It seems they were pretty interested in me, holding me for a long time while they talked. The man was standing by the stairs leading up to the back porch. Our home and beds were under the back porch, but it was a long way up to the top. The humans walked around under the porch as Mama climbed the stairs until she was at this man's shoulder. She nudged his shoulder and I heard her say, "Take him. He will be a good dog for you." I was shocked! I didn't know why Mama wanted me to leave her. I thought I was her favorite. Well, that day turned out okay because this couple gave some green paper to the lady that owned Mama and then they left. I got to stay with Mama after all, and I also got to wear one of those new collars too. I still didn't know what the collars meant.

Two weeks later, when I was five weeks old, that same couple came back. That time they took me with them in their car. I felt sad to leave Mama and my brother and sisters. I was the first to leave. But these people were so glad to have me be with them that I decided I would make the best of it. I never, ever saw Mama again.

These new humans took me to their house way, way out in the country. They kept calling me "Deacon" and said that was my new name. Well, it wasn't a new name because I never had a name before, so it was my only name. As I think about it now, I guess they wanted a "churchy" name for me because a preacher started the breed. So... Deacon it would be. Then they introduced themselves to me... the man's name was Grandpa and the lady's name was Grandma. Okay by me! Grandpa and Grandma it is!

We soon went outside on the back porch to be in the warm sun. I started walking around and, when no one was looking, I ventured too close to the edge of the porch. Boy, was I dumb! I didn't know about edges of porches and I tumbled right off to the ground. It was about a five-foot fall. "Ouch!" I said. But I stood up and walked immediately. They were so surprised that I fell and came running down the stairs to get me. Grandma picked me up and loved me, holding me close to her heart. I fell in love with her at that very moment and I knew that she loved me too. Grandpa took me and loved me also. I decided the fall was worth it because I now knew that I was loved and would be happy here for the rest of my life. I knew I was their favorite grandchild. Grandma even said so.

Now that is really saying something as I later learned that there were nine human grandchildren and eighteen great-grandchildren, plus lots of family dogs besides me. There was Rick, Brandon, Jenn, Spencer, big Melanie, Jeramy, Matthew, Claire, and little Melanie. WOW! And I'm the favorite grandchild! Grandma said we won't tell the others that I am the favorite one, but if they ever found out they would understand and be okay with it. And, whenever Grandma would talk to and play with the other dogs in the family, she would always whisper to me that I, Deacon, was the best-est of all of them. I truly believed her, too, because both Grandpa and Grandma always treated me so good.

Here is a picture of me when I was five weeks old and the other grandkids came to meet me. The little girl in the picture with me is Claire, and here she is 10 years old. Oh my! That makes her twenty-five years old now.

24
French Fries

The second day in my new home, we got into the car again. I got to ride on Grandma's lap. I hoped I would always get to ride on her lap. Boy, it was a long ride. Grandpa and Grandma talked to each other about going to the airport in Spokane, Washington, whatever that was. It seems we would meet someone there. They left me in the car as they went into the building. I didn't like being left alone. I had never been alone before in my whole life! It was scary, but somehow, I knew they would come back. I was so tired that I just fell asleep while waiting for them.

They finally came back to the car. Boy was I happy to see them! But wait! There was no one with them. What happened to them? I heard them talking that "LeRoy" (who is that?) missed his connecting flight (whatever that is) and wasn't there. It was 5pm now and they would have to wait until 11pm for him to come in on the next flight. They were upset about the wait and were worried about him. It was too far to go home and come back, so waiting was the only thing we could do.

The problem was that I was getting hungry now...really hungry! Grandma must be able to read my mind because she had brought along some food for me and got it out and fed me. Then she gave me a drink of water. They talked about being hungry too. We drove around for a little while and then Grandpa parked the car somewhere that really smelled good. There were a lot of other cars there and lots of people with dogs in their cars, too. Grandma went inside while Grandpa held me close to him and talked to me. I didn't have to stay alone this time. When Grandma came back, she had some of that good smell with her.

I know I ate dog food already, but that smell! It was so good! Grandma and Grandpa started eating what they called hamburgers and French fries. I just had to have a taste of that good smell. Finally, after what felt like forever, Grandpa gave me a bite of a French fry. YUM, YUM, YUM! I wanted more. I decided that day that I loved French fries... and I did love French fries for the rest of my life. Of course, I preferred the French fries, but only if all the meat from the hamburger was gone.

Eleven o'clock finally came and we went back to that place they called the airport. We did the same thing again; they went into the building and I stayed in the car. They apologized to me for leaving me in the car but said the law didn't allow me inside that building. The law? What was that? They said I just had to lay down and wait again. So, I did.

This became something we did over and over during my long life. I didn't mind staying in the car waiting for them, because I learned to trust that they would come back soon. And they often had a treat for me. When it was hot outside, Grandpa would leave the car running with the air conditioner on. Some people frowned and shook their heads back and forth as if they disapproved of Grandpa and Grandma leaving me in the car. I wanted to stay in the car instead of staying home alone. After all, it was my job to take care of the car. I hardly ever had to stay home alone. I loved going with them!

Well, I got off my story, didn't I? LeRoy was with them this time when they came back to the car.

He thought I was a very special puppy, too. I found out that LeRoy was Grandma's stepfather.

Over the next few days I learned that we lived on a large piece of land, still in North Idaho. Grandpa said we had 80 acres. Boy o' boy, I sure learned to love that piece of land. I saw strange animals that I wanted to chase but was told not to. There were lots of deer, elk, moose, bear, cougar, rabbits, big birds and my favorite, squirrels! Grandpa let me chase the squirrels. Mostly they were just off the front porch. Grandpa and Grandma would sit on special chairs that moved back and forth and help me see the squirrels. Grandma would use her arm and hand motions to show me which tree they were in. I never got to catch one, but it sure was fun trying. When I wasn't chasing squirrels, I was sitting in my own chair on the porch with Grams.

Here is a picture of LeRoy, Grandpa, Snoopy and me.

Early on, right after I came to my forever home, some other people came to visit. I was told their names were, Roger, Kathy, Ron and Claire. Roger and Kathy lived down the road and had a dog named Toby. Ron and his daughter, Claire brought another Jack Russell Terrier with them. His name was Snoopy. Soon, Snoopy came to live with me for a little while. I loved Snoopy. I loved to play with him. But he acted like he didn't like me very well, then all of a sudden, he would play. I finally decided he did like me but was upset that Ron and Claire left him with us. He lived with us for about a year and then eventually got to go back to his family. We remained good buddies for the rest of our lives.

Now, I might as well tell you that I finished my life on earth on November 26, 2018, and Snoopy finished his about five years before me. We are in Heaven together again now. I had such a good life that I wanted to tell everyone that would listen, so I'm writing this book from Heaven.

Snoopy taught me everything I knew that year he lived with me. He was about 17 months older than me and I looked up to him. Did you see him in the previous picture? Grandpa is holding Snoopy, too. Snoopy was my Hero. I mimicked every movement or noise that he made. We had dueling power-runs all over the house. Grandma and Grandpa let us do it as they thought it was funny and good exercise for us. There was one thing that I taught Snoopy. If I wanted him to play, I would walk up to him and side-hip-bump him. He would respond with trying to "get" me for doing that to him, and the game was on!

I also met other family Jack Russell Terriers. One named Abby belonged to Brandon, and Biggie belonged to Spencer. By the way, Biggie's full name is Biggie Smalls. He was named after a Rap singer…whatever that is. Toby wasn't a Jack Russell Terrier, but he was a good pal that lived just down the road with Roger and Kathy. He was a little BIG to me, but I finally got over being afraid of him. All of us dogs would chase squirrels together while the people would sit on the porch and watch us. We never caught even one, but it was so much fun.

We had a couple of curved trees that I could climb. Of course, the squirrels would never stay in those trees, but just jumped to another branch farther away. I loved those curved trees. Grandpa and Grandma said dogs were not supposed to climb trees. But I did!

Here is a picture of me when I was about four years old up in a tree looking for squirrels.

25

Snowbirds

Every winter we would go to Arizona. Grandpa and Grandma said we were snowbirds. I didn't really know what a snowbird was, but I couldn't see any wings, beaks or feathers on any of us, and there sure wasn't any snow there or on us, either.

We traveled a lot in the motorhome. I loved the motorhome. It was just like a house on wheels. It was a really, really big car, but with furniture, a bed and even a bathroom for the humans.

I made up a fun game for myself. I would stand up on the couch behind Grandpa while he was driving. I had my front feet on the back of his driver's seat. I would watch the oncoming traffic. The really big trucks, the ones Grandpa called 18-wheelers, would scare me as they were passing by us going in the opposite direction. I decided to be brave and

Here is a picture of me in the motorhome.

chase them. I would watch them get as close as they could and then I would run the length of the motorhome covering the couch and the table, jumping over a low divider onto the bed trying to stay up with the big truck as it whizzed by. When I reached the back of the motorhome and the truck was gone, I would go back to my position behind Grandpa and wait for the next one. It was a really fun game! Sometimes Grandma would tell me to stop, but I wouldn't. So, she would put my leash on me and then I would have to lie down and rest.

While we were snowbirds in Arizona, we rode our ATVs out in the desert. You should have seen those big eared Jack Rabbits! One very hot day, Grandma wasn't with us and Grandpa and I went out alone. Grandpa let me out of my box to go potty. He didn't put the leash on me like Grandma always did.

I saw movement under a desert bush, and I realized it was a Jack Rabbit. I took out after it. Boy, can they run fast and far! I ran and ran, darting in and out of bushes and across the hard, hot ground. My feet hurt but I didn't care; I wanted to catch that rabbit. I chased it for miles it seemed, but then suddenly I lost it. I couldn't see it anymore. I stopped and looked around me. I couldn't see Grandpa either! Suddenly I was scared.

I didn't know what to do, where to go to find Grandpa. I decided to smell the ground around me and follow my own scent back the way I came. I followed it backwards for quite a while. Then I looked up... there he was! Grandpa was on top of a mound on his ATV looking for me, calling to me.

I was so tired, so thirsty, and so scared, and yet so relieved to have found Grandpa. Grandpa was so happy to have found me that he didn't even get after me for running away after that Jack Rabbit. He gave me some water and put me in my box on the ATV. I was so happy to be back with him. I was thinking that I will never do that again. And I never did. Well, there was that deer in Idaho.

When Grandpa told Grandma about losing me for a while out there on the desert, she was mad! She told him to always put the leash on me from now on. She also shook her finger at me.

We went to a lot of neighborhood parties in the evenings. Grandpa and Grandma called them "Miller Time". I wondered what that meant. Almost everyone had a dog (or two). I noticed that the humans knew the dog's names before they knew the owner's names. Sometimes Grandma would put me on my leash and take me for a walk with a group of ladies and their dogs. There would be seven or eight of us all walking out in the middle of the quiet streets of Salome, Arizona. I preferred the private walks with only Grandma and me though, which we did almost every day.

We lived in a house in a new development called Indian Hills. Grandma and Grandpa loved that house. Therefore, I liked it too. Sometimes we would have the neighborhood over to our house for those parties called "Miller Time." Lots of dogs would come and run wild. Grandma kept me on a leash. I didn't like that, after all, it was my yard! But then again, she knew that I didn't like other dogs too well and that I liked to be the only dog in the room. She was right. I didn't like the other dogs and I would let them know that this is <u>MY</u> territory. Grandma always said to me to be nice to them and not to scare them. She said they were babies and to not hurt them. That wasn't always true... the part about them being babies, I mean. But she did always tell me that I was the best-est of all the dogs.

The neighbors liked for Grandpa to take the lead on an ATV ride in the desert and a long line of ATVs would follow us. I liked being the leader. In fact, I always scolded others if they tried to take the lead. I didn't even like Grandma to take the lead after she got her own ATV. She said she liked following Grandpa and me, that way the dust didn't get in my eyes. They were always putting my welfare first.

Here is my family on the ATV in Arizona in November 2003.

Grandpa never got lost. Well, he did when he was in Phoenix, Arizona, but never in the desert or in any wilderness land. Sometimes there were 20 ATVs following us. Grandma was always second, then the others would follow.

One time, Grandma turned her ATV over. I was so scared when I saw her pinned under her ATV.

But Grandma's son Ron saw Grandma flip over, alerted the men, and ran to help. All the men on the ride picked up her ATV and got her out. She wasn't hurt really bad, just a fractured rib, a scratch on her head and a sore leg where the weight of the ATV was holding her down. That was all. She didn't even go see a vet. Grandma continued to ride her ATV home after the fall. I laid on the bed with her after we got home. I could see that it was my job to take care of both Grandpa and Grandma. I liked having a job.

Then one day, Grandma decided that I should have another Jack Russell Terrier as a play mate, and that I should learn to share my territory. After all, I had loved having Snoopy around. She found one, named Gigi, that needed to be re-homed. Gigi was also a long-legged Jack Russell with a white coat, but hers was of the broken variety. You know, short hair with tuffs of longer hair in places. But the worst part of all was that she was a girl!

Here is a picture of Gigi.
She is not a bad looking dog,

I didn't want her to live in our family and I attacked her on arrival as she got out of the car, just to set the rules straight up front. Boy was that a mistake! She was mean!!! (Well, never mind that I attacked her first.) We found out that she was being re-homed because she was beating up on two big Labs at her other home. She was a seasoned fighter and did not want to come live with us either. She sure didn't like me, and I didn't like her. Grandma kept her for two days and then took her back. No other dog came to live with us ever again. I had Grandpa and Grandma to myself for the rest of my life, except when we would dog-sit for Ron's dogs.

Another time, while we were riding the ATVs in the desert, we saw a desert turtle. Grandpa let me get out of my box and smell that big thing (while I was on my leash this time). Another time we saw a Gila monster. Grandpa wouldn't let me near it, but it was interesting to watch from my box on the ATV. It turned colors, like yellow, then pink, and then more colors, as it slowly made its way over the desert floor. All the humans on the ride with us were thrilled to have really seen one in real life.

Grandpa was good at seeing the animals and the wildflowers. He knew the names of all of them. I could see that the Arizona neighbors all loved and respected Grandpa. He could build anything, repair anything and knew so much about wildlife and even birds.

One time, while Snoopy lived with us in Arizona, we were riding the ATVs and Snoopy spotted a cougar! He squealed and barked while Grandpa tried to stay where he could see it but not too close. It got away. I was pretty young and really don't remember it, but Grandpa likes to talk about it, and I have heard the story several times.

Grandma set up a dog agility run for me in the back yard. Grandpa built some of the things. I didn't really like it and didn't cooperate very well. I know it disappointed Grandma, but I guess I was a little spoiled. I would do it once in a while just to make her happy… if she had a treat that I liked. It didn't last long in our yard as Grandma gave it away to other dogs in the neighborhood.

Snoopy and I loved playing in the yard in Arizona.

This is a picture of Snoopy and me after we had been digging in mud!

Grandma wouldn't let us come into the house without a bath.

Here we are after our bath! I hate baths, but we do look better.

26

Life in Idaho

We loved it in Arizona, but every Spring we would go back to our forever home in Idaho. Sometimes the neighbors from Salome, Arizona would come and visit us in Idaho. Sometimes we would travel to their homes in different states. When they came here, they would bring their dogs too, dang it! Grandma said I had to share my toys and be nice to them, but always reminded me that I was the best-est of all the dogs.

One year we were dog sitting with Biggie and Cody. (Snoopy was already in Heaven.) It was Cody's first birthday and Grandpa and Grandma gave him a birthday party. Grandma made cupcakes in ice cream cones. Each one was just one bite for Cody! He was a Lab and a lot bigger than Biggie and me, so he got to eat four cupcakes and Biggie and I only got one each. Oh well, it was his birthday.

This is one of my birthday parties.

Since I was born in July, we were always in Idaho for my birthdays. They never forgot my birthday. Grandma would always bake doggie cookies and put a candle on one of them for me. I was allowed to sit on a bar stool at the breakfast bar... just like they did. Grandpa would blow the candle out for me and I got to eat the birthday cookie at the table. I know I was loved, and I loved Grandpa and Grandma back. I couldn't have had a better life anywhere else. I'm so glad they chose me.

Every year Grandma would have a big, big 4th of July party for family and friends. We did that for years and years, until Grandma got too old and it made her tired. Then we decided, as a family, to have a gathering at the Garfield Bay Park on a day that wasn't a holiday, just summertime weather. It was like a family reunion they said. I don't know what a reunion is, but I know there were a lot of people there.

My last year on earth, Grandma and Grandpa's 60th Wedding Anniversary on July 26, 2018. They used this summer party time to celebrate this wonderful time. I always got to go, but Grandma kept me on my leash. There were other dogs there too, but not all on their leashes! Oh well, I guess Grandma didn't want to lose me. I was older then and would not have run after anything, but Grandma said I had to have the leash in the park. It was the law! In my old age, I finally knew what "the law" was. It was whatever Grandma and Grandpa says it was!

Just think! I'm the favorite of all these kids! The grass was so good to scratch my back on. I guess I should have waited until after the picture was taken to roll over.

One day, Grandpa started blowing into a shiny, silver toy that he called a Harmonica. It made sharp, high-pitched noises that kind of hurt my ears a little. I decided to let Grandpa know that I didn't like it. Well, guess what! Grandpa and Grandma thought I was singing with it. They laughed and encouraged me to keep making noises. They said I was singing. Grandma would clap her hands and tell me to "sing". Well it turned out to be fun, so I did what they wanted me to do. After that I decided that when people clapped their hands I was supposed to sing. In fact, when we had the large 4th of July parties, we would all get into a large circle and everyone would clap their hands so I could sing. I was a good singer.

Sometimes in the evening when Grandpa and Grandma were sitting on the back porch, I would wander out into the big field behind the house to go see a deer or at least see how close I could get to them before they ran away. Grandpa would call me back, but sometimes, probably because I was spoiled, I didn't mind him. He would get his harmonica and start to play, trying to entice me to come back so I could sing at his feet. Sometimes I would go back, but sometimes I would just sit down where I was out in the big field and pretend that I was on a big stage and sing my heart out right there in that big field. Grandma would always clap her hands for me to sing more. Now I want you to know that I always went back to the house, but it was when I was ready to go. I could have been a better-behaved dog, but they seemed to love me anyway.

We traveled all over the United States in the motorhome or the truck sometimes. One trip to Memphis, Tennessee was one to remember. Who would have thought that the RV park that we stayed in had a problem with ticks? We only stayed overnight and the next morning when Grandpa was unhooking the motorhome, Grandma took me out to potty. We all got back in and took off down the road. It was still dark outside as we liked to get early starts.

As it was getting day light, Grandma noticed that I had a lot, and I mean LOTS of black spots on my tummy and legs. I was so uncomfortable. It was like a stinging feeling all over my tummy and legs. They decided that the dark spots were ticks and that I needed a good bath to get these bugs off of me. I was not going to argue with them over *this* bath! They were worried about theses ticks infesting the motorhome and them!

We came to a motel that accepted dogs and we stayed the rest of the day and night there to rid me of ticks. They found out that they were dog ticks and wouldn't get on humans. Grandma took all the small throw rugs out and tossed them in a dumpster so I wouldn't get more from any that were possibly in the motorhome. She vacuumed everything in there! That was an experience that I never wanted repeated. I don't think they wanted to repeat it either.

Grandpa would get sick sometimes on our long trips and Grandma would have to drive. I took care of Grandpa. It was my job. I liked taking care of him. I loved him so much.

When we traveled in the Silverado pickup truck, I liked riding on Grandma's lap. She didn't much like my running around when I would see something to get excited about. I would jump up to see cows, horses, deer or anything that I might possibly chase even though they were outside the truck. The pickup was so high that I could see a lot. I also had the whole back seat to myself if I wanted to nap. Grandma and Grandpa finally made a bed for me in the space between the seats. There was a leash (there it is again, always restraining my movements!) to keep me in the bed and not in Grandma's lap. She said it was a good thing because if we were in an accident it would be like a seat belt and keep me from going through the windshield.

She was right, because we did have a bad accident one time. All of us had our seat belts on and no one got hurt except Grandma. Her neck was broken in two places. She had to go to see the vet a lot and it took a full year and then some to get well. She always sounded funny when she talked after that. She said she lost her voice during the surgery. That's okay, I could still understand her when she talked.

Boy, I remember how that crash felt... all of a sudden, I was falling out of my box onto Grandma's lap then back and forth sideways, then BOOM! Straight down real hard. It scared me so. I was trying to get back into my bed, but I couldn't.

I got to ride in the ambulance though. That was fun! Grandma and Grandpa said they would not leave the crashed truck without me. The nice people that came with the ambulance said I could ride along with them and that Roger would come get me at the hospital. When we got to the hospital, they took Grandma and Grandpa away from me. It took a while for Roger to come get me, but the ambulance guy stayed with me until he did get there. I was so worried about Grandpa and Grandma, but finally Ron, Kristie and Kathy joined Roger and then they brought Grandpa and Grandma out to Ron's pickup to take us all home. I was so glad to see them again. I loved them so. I planned to take care of both of them. We soon got a new truck, but it was smaller. It was a Chevy Colorado.

In our travels on long trips I loved to get out and smell along the road. Grandma would put a leash on me so the traffic wouldn't hurt me. Sometimes if I was bored, I faked needing to potty, just so I could get out. It worked most of the time.

One time, Grandma gave me crackers with peanut butter inside while we were going down the road to town because I didn't eat my breakfast. I remembered exactly where we were on the road the first time, she ever gave me crackers, and then on future trips to town, each time we reached that part of the road, I would start begging for crackers. I would stare at her purse. She knew what I wanted. Grandma and I could talk to each other with our minds. She said it was telepathic talk. Sometimes she would tell me I had to wait for the crackers, but she was a pushover, easy-peasy. I always got my crackers in the end!

While in Idaho, in the fall, Grandpa would go hunting. He wouldn't let me go with him on the ATV because he said I had too much white color on me and he was hunting white tail deer. He didn't want some other hunter to mistake me for a white tail deer.

One time I had to stay home as he and Grandma went to get the deer that he had just shot so they could drag it home. He always hunted on our own property. They dragged it home, but I didn't know where they put it. When Grandma opened the door to get me, I was ready, and I ran outside to find Grandpa and the deer. I smelled the ground and took off to meet Grandpa. I ran and ran, following the smell of a deer on the ground. I got to the place where I thought Grandpa would be but neither he nor the deer were there! This was a long way from the house.

Now what?! I thought, "I'm in trouble for sure." I must have missed something, so, I retraced my tracks like I did on the Arizona desert when I got lost chasing the rabbit. I made it halfway back to the house when all of a sudden, I heard the ATV coming towards me. Grandpa was on it and I was sure he would be mad at me. But again, he was just so glad to have found me safe that he just helped me get into my box on the ATV and we went back to the house. Of course, Grandma was ready with a scolding. I got to see the deer, too, as it was down on the ground waiting to be hung up and processed. It seems that when I left the house if I had turned left instead of right, I would have gone straight to Grandpa and the deer behind the shop. I decided to never do that again. But actually, that was the last deer that Grandpa ever got. He had to stop hunting after that, "because of his health," he said.

I took my job of taking care of Grandpa seriously. I could see that Grandpa was losing weight and needed to eat more. Besides, if he ate, I ate! So, when Grandma would start putting plates on the table or even just start to cook... I would go directly to Grandpa and tell him to come to the table, NOW! I think my timing was off sometimes and it was too soon for him to come, but since I wasn't sure, I insisted he come, NOW. I would bark and bark directly at him. Sometimes he would come, but I think he was watching Grandma to know when to come instead of me. I was just trying to take care of him. I loved him. I was just doing my job. They knew that and loved me anyway.

27

My Last Days

I lived a long time, 15 years and 4 months. In fact, in dog years, they told me I was 105 years old. I was sick inside for at least four years. I had a tumor in my colon, not cancer, but still it made me bleed when I pooped. Grandpa and Grandma would always wipe my butt for me so I wouldn't get blood on the carpet. Sometimes I did, but Grandma would just clean it up. She even made up special wipes especially for me out of toilet paper. There was a supply by each door to make it convenient.

They watched me to see if I was hurting or not. I was… some, but I wanted to stay here on earth to take care of Grandpa and Grandma until they died. Then I would go, too. So, I didn't always let them know when I was hurting. But, Grandma could tell most of the time. She would gently rub my tummy and make it feel better.

Then one day I got so sick, I couldn't see right. I couldn't stand up or walk. When I tried to walk, I just kept going in circles, always to my left. I later found out that I couldn't see because my eyeballs were actually shaking, like bouncing, throwing off my focus. Grandma took me to see the vet. I remembered him; I remembered that smell. That was the place that I was taken when they cut off my tail, my toes (dewclaws) and gave me shots… yes, shots all my life! He said I was having a stroke, whatever that was. He said if I made it through the first few days, I likely would likely recover, maybe even 100%.

Did he mean that I might die? I wasn't sure how I felt about that.

This happened on Easter Sunday of 2017. Grandma and Grandpa took really good care of me. Grandma was a Registered Nurse when she worked, before she retired, so she knew about strokes. I have to be honest with you folks… I really thought about going to live in Heaven at that time, but I didn't want to leave Grandpa. I would be leaving my job of taking care of him. After the first few days I decided to live instead of dying. I'm so glad I did.

The vet said that dogs recover from strokes faster than humans. It took me about two months and then I was my old self again. I recovered 100% with Grandma and Grandpa's help. They would do physical therapy on me by holding me up with my harness so I could practice walking again. Grandma placed my water dish and food where I could get to them easily. You see, I couldn't hold my head up right for a while. It seemed to stay sideways and was

Here is a picture of me when I was just getting better about holding up my head. *See how my head is not straight? I just couldn't hold it up right. I felt weak and sick.*

so heavy to hold up. I loved Grandma and Grandpa for all their love, concern, and care.

About a year and one-half after the stroke, the tumor inside me continued to grow bigger and it was closing off my bowels. It made it hard for me to poop. I was sick. I was hurting and Grandpa and Grandma had a good talk with me. They said it would be okay for me to go on without them and find a good place for us to all be together again in Heaven. They said Snoopy was there and would show me around. We could play together again, and they would come as soon as they could. Grandma said I could visit them from Heaven and even talk to them. They would be watching for me to visit.

I told them that I was ready to go. I was tired of the pain and not being able to poop right anymore. They took me to the vet on November 26, 2018, and Grandma stayed with me until I went to sleep forever… at least for here on earth. Grandma told me I could go home with them in my new spiritual body if I wanted to. Of course, I wanted to!!! And I did go! Grandma could see me in the truck with them.

I also went to see my dog buddies while in my spiritual body just before my heart stopped beating. I went to their house in Bonners Ferry, Idaho to say goodbye to Cody, Quill, Sophia, Odin, Biggie and especially Saige. I loved playing with Saige. She was the only girl dog that I had ever liked. They were all sad that I wouldn't be at my house out in the country anymore when they came to visit. And then my heart stopped, and I was with Snoopy.

Grandma and Grandpa were sad for a very long time, but they shouldn't cry and be sad because I'm okay now. I don't hurt anymore and I'm with

Snoopy, just like they said I would be. And that is wonderful! Snoopy and I are young puppies again. I walk up to him and give him that side hip bump to get him to play with me. We run together. Talk about running... We do power runs all over Heaven! The Angels laugh at us and love us. We are happy here.

That is why I wanted to write this book, so I could tell Grandpa and Grandma that I had a wonderful life with them, and I loved that they picked me to be their puppy for fifteen years. I loved my life and I loved taking care of them. We made a great family!

*Grandma took this picture the night before
I went to see Snoopy in Heaven.*

So, take your time Grandpa and Grandma. Snoopy and I will be here waiting on this side of the bridge for you. We'll have a great big party when you get here.

Oh say! I watched you spread my ashes, Grandma, out there where Grandpa suggested. It

was a perfect place because that is where I used to chase squirrels. I loved that! Thank You!
 I love you Grandpa and Grandma.

The following is a tribute to Deacon by Grandpa:

I had a little white dog
His name was Deacon

He and I roamed the woods together
Over the hills and down the valleys

We chased the squirrels and the moose
for fun together

Now he has crossed the river
and is on the other side

I am sure he is waiting for me
to come and be by his side

To explore the wonderments of the mountains,
valleys and dells, side by side again.
Grandpa
(Norman T. Campbell)

Acknowledgements

First, I must acknowledge my husband Norm, and our wonderful pet, a Jack Russell Terrier, named Deacon. This book would not have been written without their love, patience and an ability to share information about their health journeys which led me to experience anticipatory grief over and over, even though I had experienced it with other family members before them.

Second, I want to acknowledge my son, Ron, for his contribution of commenting on certain ideas in the book and his beautiful photograph so appropriately used for the cover.

And finally, though not least by any means, a big thank you goes to my grandson, Rick and my friend Linda for allowing me to use their poems, which express the emotions that anticipatory grief can help bring to us an understanding of where we are on our Soul's journey.

Bibliography

Alexander, Eben, "Map of Heaven" (New York, NY: Simon and Schuster, 2014)

Barnum, Melanie, "The Book of Psychic Symbols" (Woodbury, Minnesota: Llewellyn Publications, 2016)

Byock, Ira, "Dying Well: Peace and Possibilities at the End of Life" (New York, NY: Riverhead Books, 1997)

Campbell, Ron, Pastor, "What Does It Mean to Fear God?" (Small Group Disciples Online Blog, www.smallgroupdisciples.com, August 20, 2018)

Campbell, Virginia, "Spiritual Reflections… I Tried, God Helped" Bonner's Ferry, ID: Profotofix Publishing, 2016)

Caputo, Teresa, "You Can't Make This Stuff Up" (New York, NY: Atria Books, 2015)

Chopra, Deepak, "Reinventing the Body, Resurrecting the Soul" (New York, NY: Harmony Books, 2009)

Choquette, Sonia, "The Answer is Simple, Love Yourself, Live Your Spirit" (USA: Hay House, 2008)

De Pape, Baptist, "The Power of the Heart" (New York: Simon and Schuster, 2014)

Dillard, Sherrie, "You Are a Medium" (Woodbury, MN: Llewellyn LTD, 2017)

Doka, Kenneth, PhD & Davidson, Joyce, "Living with Grief When Illness is Prolonged" (Washington, DC: Taylor and Francis, 1997)

Dyer, Wayne, PhD, "Change Your Thoughts… Change Your Life" (USA: Hay House, 2007)

Frankl, Viktor, "Man's Search for Meaning" (Boston, Mass: Beacon Press, 1992)

Griswold, Trudy, "Angelspeake online Newsletter" (angelspeake.com, June 11, 2018)

Hawkins, David, "Power VS Force" (USA: Hay House, 2002)

Hicks, Esther & Jerry, "Ask and It is Given" (USA: Hay House, 2004)

Holland, John, "Bridging Two Realms" (USA: Hay House, 2018)

Howe, Linda, "Discover Your Soul's Path Through the Akashic Records" (USA: Hay House, 2015)

Howe, Linda, "Healing Through the Akashic Records" (Boulder, CO: Sounds True, 2016)

James, William, "The Varieties of Religious Experience" (New York, NY: Barnes and Noble Classics, 1902)

Kumar, Sameet M, PhD, "Grieving Mindfully" (Oakland, CA: New Harbinger Publications, Inc., 2005)

Lintermans, Gloria & Stolzman, Marilyn PhD, "The Healing Power of Grief" (Wisconsin: Champion Press, LTD, 2006)

Moss, Maureen, "The Nature of Bliss" (Ashland, OR: Sidney House Publishing, 2002)

Moss, Maureen, "Commitment to Love" (Ashland, OR: Sidney House Publishing, 2004)

Myss, Caroline, "Why People Don't Heal and Why They Can" (New York, NY: Three Rivers Press, 1997)

Nelson, Tony L, "Crazy Life, Navigating Through Life's Disruptions Without Losing Your Faith" (New York, NY: Morgan James Publishing, 2017)

Roman, Sanaya, "Spiritual Growth" (Tiburon, CA: HJ Kramer, Inc., 1989)

Russell, Bertrand, "Why I Am Not a Christian"; copyright by George Allen and Un Win LTD, (New York, NY: Simon and Schuster, 1957)

Singer, Michael A, "The Untethered Soul" (Oakland, CA: New Harbinger Publications, Inc., 2007)

Schwartz, Robert, "Your Soul's Gift" (USA: Whispering Winds Press, 2012)

Tipping, Colin, "Radical Forgiveness… Making Room for the Miracle" (Marietta, GA: Global Thirteen Publications, 2002)

Tolle, Eckhart, "Stillness Speaks" (Vancouver Canada: Namaste Publishing, 2003)

Tolle, Eckhart, "A New Earth…Awakening to Your Life's Purpose" (New York, NY: Plume Book Publishing, 2005)

Vanzant, Iyanla, "Until Today" (New York, NY: Simon and Schuster, 2001)

Virtue, Doreen and Van Praagh, James, "How to Heal a Grieving Heart" (USA: Hay House, 2013)

Williamson, Marianne, "The Gift of Change" (San Francisco, CA: Harper Collings Publisher, 2004)

CPSIA information can be obtained
at www.ICGtesting.com
Printed in the USA
LVHW062144170723
752733LV00042B/736